Eu … s

...then I am in a culture where I can breathe.
Raymond Williams

For Gwyn A. Williams:
'We live if we act...'

welsh
Europeans

John Osmond

seren

Seren
is the book imprint of
Poetry Wales Press Ltd
Wyndham Street, Bridgend
Wales

A Cataloguing in Publication record for this title
is available from the British Library CIP Office

ISBN 1-85411-156-6

Seren works with the financial support of the
Arts Council of Wales.

Printed in Palatino by
WBC Book Manufacturers, Bridgend

Contents

Acknowledgements

My first debt is to Lindsay Patterson, editor of the journal *Scottish Affairs*, who commissioned an earlier version of the opening chapter of this book, which appeared in *Scottish Affairs* No.11, Spring 1995. Working on this commission made me see many of the contradictions that form the linkages between the essays.

An earlier version of Chapter Two, 'Living in Quangoland', appeared in *Planet* No. 110 (April/May 1995). Chapter Three, 'Democracy in the Balance', is based on research of the same title I undertook with Mari James of the Centre for Advanced Social Studies (CASS) at the University Wales College of Cardiff in the autumn of 1994, commissioned from CASS by Unison Cymru/Wales. An earlier version of Chapter Four, 'Viceroys on the Make', appeared in *Planet* No, 105 (June/July 1994). Chapter Six, 'Partnership and Economic Renewal', is based on research I undertook with Professor Kevin Morgan of the Department of Regional and Town Planning, University of Wales College of Cardiff, for Business in the Community Wales and Community Enterprise Wales during 1995. Chapter Eight, 'Unitary Britain and Regional Europe', is based on a paper I presented at the Fifth Freudenstadt Seminar, 'Networking Europe', organised by the University of Tubingen and the Friedrich Ebert Foundation, in Baden Wurttemberg in June 1995. I am grateful to Professor Christopher Harvie, of the University of Tubingen, for the invitation.

Robin Reeves, Mari James, Kevin Williams and Kevin Morgan all read early drafts of the material and made many helpful suggestions. Andy Corrigan, Dafydd Williams and Paul Griffiths were essential sources of statistics and information. Tom Nairn was always at the end of the telephone. Gwerfyl Hughes Jones helped with translations. I am grateful to Mick Felton and his colleagues at Seren who very rapidly decided to take on this project. As ever my wife Alphie provided editorial advice and constant support.

John Osmond
Penarth
September 1995

INTRODUCTION

Two central themes connect the essays in this book. The first is a widening gulf between the government of Wales and the ability of the Welsh people to have any real say in how they are governed. The second, intimately related to the first, is an increasing contradiction between Welshness on the one hand and Britishness on the other. For some generations the Welsh have lived reasonably comfortably inside a dual identity in which Welshness and Britishness have both found expression. One has been more salient than the other according to time, occasion and circumstance. Living with the duality is becoming less easy, however, because the meaning of Britishness is being drained away. It has been a long process, but in the 1990s it is accelerating as the European dimension of our affairs gathers momentum.

The main argument of the book is that we now have a route along which we can resolve these contradictions. It is no coincidence that in the 1990s an opportunity to create Welsh democratic institutions is occurring at the same time as the Welsh are becoming European in a national as well as cultural sense. In the past we have been Welsh British subjects. In the future we can become Welsh European citizens.

Questions of identity — what it means to be Welsh — underpin this debate. Certainly where nationality is concerned, identity is always produced in relation to specific circumstances, to real interests and institutions. One confusion that arises is that there are as many Welsnesses as there are communities in Wales. Yet if we can give them democratic expression we can discover a unity in this diversity. We can feel directly, in an intimate personal way, that Wales is indeed, as it always has been, a community of communities.

In the process of discovery it is instructive, though not always obvious, to start at the beginning. In my grandmother's house in Cardiff when I was growing up through the 1950s, I have a vivid memory of staring for what seemed like hours at two pictures celebrating British valour in the Napoleonic wars. They were prints of etchings taken from tapestries that still hang in the House of Lords. One showed Nelson slumped in the arms of fellow officers on the deck of the Victory at the Battle of Trafalgar, even more glorious because of his imminent death. The other, which we have hanging on our own wall today, shows Wellington meeting the German general Blucher at Waterloo, clinching the battle that destroyed Napoleon and established Britain as the foremost European power for a century.

These pictures fascinated me. In part, no doubt, it was the blood-thirsty detail of the drawings that held my eye — men dead and dying over abandoned cannon and collapsed horses, cavalry charges still underway in the distance. But underlying their immediate drama, and reinforced by the Victorian atmosphere of the house, was a strong feeling that here was a source. Here, it felt, was something my family held important, something that, indeed, had made us what we were.

My family had grown momentarily prosperous on the back of the rapid expansion of Cardiff as a coal exporting port around the turn of the century. This was the moment when south Wales was integrated most thoroughly into the British imperial project, providing the coal that fuelled the British fleet. Up to the 1950s that identity had been carried forward by the two World Wars when the Germans not the French were the enemy. 'The only good German is a dead German', my grandfather on the other side of the family often told me. But looking at those pictures I sensed that the trajectory had begun much earlier. Since then my child's instinct has been confirmed and filled-out by a reading of history, for example Linda Colley's *Britons — Forging the Nation 1707-1837*.[1]

A professor at Yale University, Linda Colley describes herself as half-Welsh and half-English. Yet her book tells how those elements which went into the making of the British, and which still grip the British imagination, are rapidly losing relevance. As she says, 'God is no longer British, and Providence no longer smiles'. War combined with religion, trade and Empire to 'invent' Britain following the union of Scotland with England and Wales in 1707. Seven wars against the French followed, lasting more than 40 years until final victory at Waterloo in 1815. Above all, however, it was Protestantism that fused the English, Welsh and Scots (the Catholic Irish were excluded) together despite their many cultural differences.

The Empire created as a result of these religious wars convinced Victorians of Britain's providential destiny. God had entrusted Britons with a global destiny as a testimony to their status as the Protestant Israel. The contemporary problem for this vision is not merely that the Empire has gone, leaving Britain 'without a role'. Protestantism itself is now only a residual part of our culture, no longer able to define itself against a predominantly Catholic Europe. Even more of a problem is that, being part of the European Union, Britain cannot define itself against the European powers at all. As Professor Colley says, 'Whether it likes it or not, Britain is fast becoming part of an increasingly federal Europe'. It is as part of that process that we in Wales are becoming Welsh Europeans.

Of course, we have always been Welsh though what that has been meant has forever been disputed. We have lived too close to the English for it to be otherwise. It was they, or rather the Saxons that gave us the name, which actually means foreigners. Yet in the continual disputation there is a kind of confirmation.

The Welsh are a people certainly. Are we a nation? The Scots do not worry about that question in the same way. As that remarkable document *A Claim of Right for Scotland* put it in 1988, 'Much ink is wasted on the question whether the Scots are a nation. Of course they are'.[2] We ask the question with more force in Wales because we lack the institutional infrastructure that underpins Scottish identity. It is institutions that define a state and create a sense of citizenship. Since the 1950s Wales has been busy building its own institutions, with the critical moment being the creation of the Welsh Office in 1964. The arguments that took place in the decade leading up to that achievement are highly relevant for our position today and some of them are discussed in Chapter 10. In any event Welsh political, economic and cultural institutions have multiplied so rapidly since then that it is now possible to talk in terms of a Welsh state, albeit one that is bureaucratic and not yet democratic. It can accurately be said in the 1990s that the Welsh are a people struggling to become a nation by progressively establishing their own institutions.

As a people who in the past have lacked state institutions of their own, the Welsh have been instinctively tribal. When Welsh people meet it can be guaranteed that, if not the first, the second or third question will be 'Where are you from originally?' — meaning, where within the boundaries of Wales is your source community.

In my own case I was born and brought up in Abergavenny in

the border country of northern Gwent. It was home in the same period, too, for John Barnie whose autobiographical volume *The Confirmation* accurately describes what it was like growing up there in the 1950s.[3] This volume of prose and poetry has to be picked through carefully to find traces of Welshness — in that gradation, from 'not very Welsh' to 'very Welsh' so commonly deployed in Wales. What other mainstream nationality in the British Isles has such an attribute applied to it, indicating that its identity is a question of degree rather than being a straightforward category? Of course, a person may be regarded as 'very Scottish' perhaps 'very Irish', or even 'very English'. However, such descriptions generally denote a type of Scottishness, Irishness, or Englishness rather than call into question the essence of what it actually is to be those things. It is not so in Wales. Here for some 'Welshness' begins west of Cardiff and north of Pontypridd. For these, if Welshness resides in the south-east it does so with a perpetual question mark hanging over it. In this pantheon, and despite it being traditionally described as the 'gateway to Wales' there is an especially large question mark hovering over the town of Abergavenny.

And still it produces a man like John Barnie, whose identification with Wales, particularly through his editorship of the magazine *Planet*, has become his life's mission. How so? The answer is not immediately obvious in *The Confirmation*. Nonetheless it can divined by a discerning and imaginative eye. We are talking here of the 1940s and 1950s, a world that in time is very near, but because of the ever-gathering pace of historical change, already lost forever, except in the memory. At one point John Barnie pauses to describe the border character of this closed-in world:

> To the east the hedgerowed fields of England blazed green, fading into a distant hazy blue; to the west ridge on ridge of the Black Mountains, rising like slow Atlantic waves, jostling in the endless thrust of Earth, moving with the flotsam of farms and animals.

There is an intimation here that both sides are in some way foreign territory, England to the east and Wales to the west. The same point has been famously made by Raymond Williams, speaking about his upbringing in nearby Pandy,

> There was a curious sense in which we could speak of

> both Welsh and English as foreigners, as 'not us'.[4]

It is interesting that *The Confirmation* contains much of the flavour of Raymond Williams' novel *Border Country*. One difference is that Raymond Williams was writing from outside, rather than inside the town which in his novel he calls Gwenton. At the school we all three attended, King Henry VIII Grammar, the boys were divided into two houses — Oppidans and Rusticans. John Barnie and I were Oppidans. Raymond Williams was decidedly a Rustican. Nonetheless, and this is a general characteristic of Wales, the country was always close at hand. In *The Confirmation* there is a continual sense of being able to view the town and its people from above, a feeling of being cradled in the Earth and thereby part of it. For me this is the point from which our Welsh particularity, and our special sense of place, emanates. And I think John Barnie gets it from the same source, as when he describes his main character, himself, walking at night in the hills above the town:

> When he reached the end of the ridge he stopped again. There below were the lights of the town, like a crowd gathering and milling with sparkling torches.

In this universe people are viewed simultaneously from a perspective of annonymity and familiarity. Throughout *The Confirmation* there is an ever-felt presence of 'neighbours' and not in the narrow sense description of the ubiquitous Antipodean soap opera. Raymond Williams often touched on this theme when describing the kind of stable community experience that formed him, and gave him a certain specific identity in opposition to outside forces. On one occasion he amplified what he meant by recalling a lecture he attended as a student at Cambridge, given by Professor L.C. Knights on the meaning of the word 'neighbour' in Shakespeare:

> He said the word indicated something that no twentieth century person can understand, because it signified a whole sense of obligations and recognitions over and above the mere fact of physical proximity. F.R. Leavis was leaning against the wall, nodding vigorously, and everybody was saying yes, in the twentieth century nobody understands the meaning of 'neighbour'. Well

> I got up, straight from Pandy, so to speak, and said I knew perfectly well what 'neighbour', in that full sense, meant.[5]

Of course, the experience of community in the Wales of the 1940s and 1950s and that of the 1990s is immensely different. Horizons have both widened and narrowed. The so-called 'global village' is one perspective, witnessed by the broadcast messages beamed into every home. Equally the kind of neighbourliness affirmed by Raymond Williams has been eroded by an urban culture that has affected Wales along with the rest of Britain, though not perhaps as much.

These are not the only changes, however. Over the past half century places like Abergavenny, as with the whole of Gwent and Glamorgan, have been drawn into a more mature relationship with Wales as a country. No longer, I think, would a young person growing up in south-eastern Wales — even in the border country of Gwent — say, as did Raymond Williams, John Barnie, and myself, that they feel apart from both Wales and England. In travelling time London is much nearer today. But in other respects, in terms of cultural affinities and an immediate shared past, it is much further away. And by the kind of paradox that is defining modern Wales, places like Dublin, Edinburgh, Brussels, Paris, Barcelona and Stuttgart can today be as near in cultural terms as London.

Such paradoxes, often straight contradictions, provide connecting themes for the essays in this book. The opening and closing chapters view the terrain largely from the perspective of the Labour movement. Because it occupies such a central position in Welsh life the way it is grappling with the contradictions that are the main themes of the book is especially important. The second and third chapters deal with the democratic dilemma. The Welsh Quango State has grown to the large extent at the expense of local government. It is a development that has done most to place the issue of democratic institutions at the Welsh level on the political agenda. The following two chapters deal with the democratic question in terms of two contrasting, indeed contradictory personalities, John Redwood and Ron Davies. The former ran Wales without a Welsh mandate, while the latter had the mandate but was powerless to rule.

At the centre of the book are chapters dealing with the economy and broadcasting. Wales in the 1990s cannot be understood unless the extent of the economic transformation that is underway is appreciated. The most important aspect of the change, so far as the themes of the book are concerned, is that it is happening to a great extent independently of the rest of the British economy. Inward investment and the growth of new manufacturing industries are taking place less in a British setting, but as much if not more in a European and global milieu. The same is true of broadcasting where the pressures for an English language television channel and more autonomy for BBC Wales in particular, are being driven by the demands of European and global broadcasting.

The Welsh are becoming European citizens in a changing Europe. Towards the end of the book two chapters deal with the emerging Europe of the Regions within which there is hope that Wales will find a place in the coming century.

Because it is such a fragmented and often marginalised society, Wales is more prone than most to seemingly never-ending, and often bizarre paradoxes and contradictions. They constantly recur in Welsh life. In the media, for instance, three-quarters of the Welsh people have to rely mainly on television programmes emanating from London. Meanwhile, a quarter have access to their own dedicated channel, originating from Cardiff. The reasons for this are well known, but it remains a paradox. To pursue the example, many among the monoglot English majority reject even the relatively small number of programmes directed at them from Cardiff. How else can we interpret the fact that so many television aerials in south-east Wales are pointed at English transmitters?

As with personal life, so with nations, such contradictions are difficult to resolve. There is often no choice but to live inside them. Nonetheless, as was said at the opening, we in Wales now have an opportunity to translate the two central contradictions afflicting Welsh life into formations that are less demobilising. Raymond Williams was acutely conscious of contradictions as a defining characteristic of the Welsh condition. As he put it in 1984, writing at a particularly low point for the aspirations described in this book:

> Many of the things that happened, over centuries, to the Welsh are now happening, in decades, to the

> English ... Of course the surviving power of England — the specific power of its ruling and political class — still presses heavily on Wales as on other marginalised communities, including many of the regions of England itself. But at many levels, from the new communal nationalisms and regionalisms to the new militant particularisms of contemporary industrial conflict, the flow of contemporary politics is going beyond the modes of all the incorporated ideologies and institutions.
>
> The Welsh, of course, have been inside these cross pressures for much longer than the English. And as a result we have had to learn that we need to solve the real contradictions between nationality and class, and between local well-being and the imperatives of a large-scale system. Consequently, we may be further along the road to a relevant if inevitably painful contemporary social consciousness.[6]

In the 1990s Raymond Williams' legacy is making an immense contribution to the construction of a relevant and contemporary social consciousness, as a reading of this book will testify. It was Raymond Williams who in the 1970s clearly saw the route through the maze of identity conflicts between Welshness on the one hand and Britishness on the other that dogged the politics of that frustrating decade. It was he who offered us the idea that we could find a culture in which we could breathe by re-making ourselves once more, but this time as Welsh Europeans.

NOTES

1. Linda Colley, Britons — *Forging the Nation 1707-1837* (Yale: Yale University Press, 1992).
2. John Barnie, *The Confirmation* (Llandysul: Gomer Press, 1993).
3. Owen Dudley Edwards (ed.) *A Claim of Right for Scotland* (a volume of essays including the 1988 document) (Edinburgh: Polygon, 1989.
4. Raymond Williams, *Politics and Letters* (London: New Left Books, 1979), p.26.
5. *Ibid.* p.67.
6. Raymond Williams, 'Wales and England', in John Osmond (ed.) *The National Question Again*, Llandysul: Gomer Press, 1985, pp.29-30.

CONTRADICTIONS OF WELSH POLITICS

Welsh politics revolve around a contradiction that while the Labour Party consistently wins a majority of seats and nearly half the vote, more often than not the Conservatives rule Wales on the basis of the support they achieve in southern England. This has been the case for much of this century. During most of the time the contradiction has quietly festered. In the latest phase since 1979, however, and especially in the 1990s, Conservative arrogance has reached new heights and pushed a resolution of the contradiction to centre stage.

The contradiction has been sharply brought into focus since the 1992 general election as the Conservatives have plumbed new depths in unpopularity. The party were beaten by Plaid Cymru into third place in the 1994 Euro-elections (see Table 1). In the Islwyn by-election, in February 1995, the Conservative candidate lost his deposit, trailing fourth behind Labour, Plaid Cymru and the Liberal Democrats. A week later an opinion poll registered just 12 per cent support for the Conservatives (the unadjusted figure was 8 per cent).

Much of Welsh life and government is now controlled by the Welsh Office. When it was first established, in 1964, it had few functions and little financial clout. Over thirty years that has changed. Today the Welsh Office controls virtually every aspect of Welsh political administration. Its civil servants have increased from two hundred to more than two thousand. From just £200m its annual budget has expanded to nearly £7 billion which is approaching 70 per cent of public spending in Wales.

More often than not the Welsh Office rules through appointed Quangos like the Welsh Development Agency, Wales Tourist Board and Higher Education Funding Council. These bodies have doubled in number to more than eighty since 1979. They employ some sixty thousand people. If the local Quango state is included, with such agencies as the 102 housing associations, 22 local hospital trusts, and the 26 governing bodies of the Further Education Colleges, then the number of appointed bodies runs

Table 1: WELSH ELECTION RESULTS AND OPINION POLLS
Figures give % poll followed by number of seats in brackets

Cymru	Labour	Conservative	Lib Dem	Plaid
1987 General Election	45.1 (24)	29.5 (8)	17.9 (3)	7.3 (3)
1992 General Election	49.5 (27)	28.6 (6)	12.4 (1)	9.0 (4)
March 1994 BBC Wales Opinion poll	60	16	9	13
June 1994 Euro-Election	55.9 (5)	14.6 (0)	8.7 (0)	17.1 (0)
Feb 1995 BBC Wales Opinion Poll	66	12	8	13

General elections and Euro-elections cannot be easily compared, not least because of differential turn-out. Nevertheless, a comparison can be made by examining how much of their 1992 vote the parties mobilised in 1994. According to figures produced by Denis Balsom, warden of the Gregynog University of Wales Study Centre, this reveals the following percentages:

% Mobilised				
Wales	61.3	27.7.	37.9	103.1
North Wales seat	62.2	24.7	33.2	142.3

to more than three hundred. Welsh Quangoland now has equivalent spending power and is undoubtedly more influential than elected local government.

Since 1979 this Welsh government machine has pushed through policies for the economy, education and the health service that are far from congenial to mainstream Welsh political opinion. As a result the Wales Labour Party is finding new resolve in its commitment to establishing a Welsh Assembly that would ensure that whatever party was in power at Westminster, a majority of Wales representatives would have their hands on the levers of Welsh Office power. In response the Conservatives are insisting that Labour's plans are threatening the integrity of the United Kingdom.

THE POLITICS OF CONFRONTATION

In the past, Conservative Secretaries of State for Wales have generally kept a low profile on the constitution, not wishing to stir up controversy in a territory where they lack a mandate. During his tenure in office from 1993-5, however, John Redwood seized on the question. At the 1994 Conservative Party Conference, for instance, he constantly drew attention to the Home Rule 'threat'. In a platform speech he said it would lead to an English backlash, loss of cash from Whitehall and fewer Welsh MPs at Westminster. And he told a fringe meeting of the Conservative Way Forward Group that nationalists who want a 'Europe of the Regions' should remember that Welsh was not an official language of the European Union.[1]

The political views and personality of John Redwood did a great deal to focus discontent. His immediate predecessors, Peter Walker and David Hunt, though also representing English constituencies, went down less badly, in part because their policy approach was markedly different, and certainly different in tone, to the way more Thatcherite policies were applied in England. Peter Walker was quite open about his emollient brand of Conservatism being applied in Wales as an experiment. This was the source of his well-publicised *Initiative* to regenerate the Welsh Valleys, a re-packaging of a scheme originally launched by his predecessor Nicholas Edwards. Looking back on his tenure at the Welsh Office between 1987 and 1990 Walker contrasted his approach with the Thatcherite reliance on free-market forces across the border:

> What we achieved in Wales as a result of close government co-operation with industry, councils and trade unions does underscore the weakness of our post-war performance in the rest of the country ... Britain, with its free trade attitude belonging to another century, adopted under Margaret an arms-length relationship between government and industry.[2]

John Redwood, on the other hand, was uncompromisingly Thatcherite, which he demonstrated in a series of policies on education, industry, Europe and local government, not to say his well publicised attack on single mothers. When he was appointed in May 1993, Opposition politicians did not hide their dismay. 'The new viceroy Mr Redwood is the last straw,' said the Welsh Liberal Democrat leader, Montgomery MP Alex Carlile. 'To impose an Englishman with views so at odds with the people of Wales is dangerously patronising.' John Redwood's role in changing the tone, if not the substance, of Welsh Office rule is explored in Chapter 4.

A paradox of the Conservative tenure at the Welsh Office since 1979 is the extent to which an all-Wales level of administration has been expanded and elaborated, albeit bureaucratic rather than democratic government. For, although the power of the Welsh Office and the Quangos has been extended to some extent at the expense of autonomous local government, it has served to entrench an institutional sense of Welsh identity. This has been articulated largely through the politics of reaction.

A cutting edge has been provided by the increasingly partisan political appointments made to the Quangos. For example, Ian Grist, who lost his Cardiff North seat to Labour at the 1992 election became chairman of South Glamorgan Health Authority not long afterwards. Beata Brookes, the former Conservative MEP for North Wales, was re-appointed chair of the Welsh Consumer Council in 1994.

Invariably, leading figures on the more powerful Quangos running Wales have Conservative connections. The Chairman of both the Welsh Development Agency and the Development Board for Rural Wales, David Rowe-Beddoe, was a member of the Conservatives Abroad Strategy Committee in the run-up to the 1992 general election and also chairman of its branch in Monaco where he has a home. These positions were made clear on his curriculum vitae presented to the Welsh Office at the time of his appointment in July 1993. Later John Redwood claimed he had been unaware of these connections.

However, it is not just a question of such appointments having a party political flavour. Rather it is the way the same personalities keep cropping up time and again. The lack of accountability, and denial of responsibility, that results from this intermeshed network of influence is exposed in Chapter 2. Welsh Quangoland has provided the backcloth for an important shift in Welsh politics in the 1990s. It has engendered a confrontational atmosphere in which the traditional disputes between the Opposition parties in the Commons, especially between Plaid Cymru and Labour, have tended to be overlain by a common outrage against the Conservatives. Interestingly, this has taken on a Welsh/English dimension as well with, for the first time for more than a generation, Labour politicians regularly referring to the Conservatives as Unionists. One of John Redwood's main achievements during his brief sojourn in Wales may turn out to have been to encourage Welsh Labour politicians to take fresh pride in their national roots.

THE TORY STEAMROLLER

Another key dimension of Welsh politics in the 1990s has been the reorganisation of local government forced through Westminster against the combined opposition of Labour, Liberal Democrats and Plaid Cymru. This has presented a further paradox since, though the Opposition parties were at least formally opposed to what the Conservatives were doing, there is no doubt that the creation of a single tier of 22 new authorities, to replace the present 8 counties and 37 districts, has been extremely influential in placing a Welsh Assembly or Parliament back on the Welsh political agenda. Indeed, so much was this the case that, behind-the-scenes, a number of pro-devolution Welsh MPs, especially from the Labour side, worked hard to ease the passage of the legislation through Parliament during 1993-4.

There is general agreement among the Opposition parties that an all-Wales body is more acceptable if there is a single-tier of local government below it. There is a common perception, too, that creating a single tier in advance of devolution will help considerably in promoting the argument for constitutional reform. Moreover, there is a recognition that it will also remove many vested interests in the shape of some Labour county councillors whose predecessors were so influential in campaigning against devolution in the 1970s.

Nonetheless, before the reorganisation was approved by the Westminster Parliament, there was much ritualised opposition. Arguably this debate contributed as much as tendentious Quango appointments to the polarisation of Welsh politics in the 1990s. Nowhere was it more clearly seen than in the wrangle over Parliamentary procedure in March 1994 to allow the Welsh local government reorganisation Bill to pass from the floor of the House of Commons to Committee. To achieve this the Government had to suspend Standing Order No 86 of the House of Commons. This procedural convention, unique to Wales, provides that 'for the consideration of any public bill relating exclusively to Wales, the committee shall be so constituted as to include all Members sitting for constituencies in Wales.'

The Standing Order was established in 1907, in the wake of the 1906 general election when the Conservatives were completely wiped out in Wales. It was a gesture by the triumphant Liberals aimed at enshrining Wales's national identity. This was pointed out during the debate on its suspension by the Cardiff Central Labour MP Jon Owen Jones, who before he was elected in 1992 was chairman of the Campaign for a Welsh Assembly, now the Parliament for Wales Campaign. He quoted from Hansard eighty-seven years earlier when, in the debate establishing the Standing Order, the Conservative Member for Gravesend, Sir Gilbert Parker, remarked, 'Behind the proposals of the Prime Minister is a process of devolution ... intended to lead up to the larger policy.'

The Standing Order also provided that the size of a Committee could not exceed 50. Given there were 32 Opposition MPs representing Welsh constituencies, unless it had been suspended the Conservatives would have lost their majority when it came to reorganising Welsh local government. To circumvent this they decided the Committee should be made up of 28 members, with 15 drawn from the Government's side. Nine English Conservatives were drafted in to shore up the six Welsh Conservative MPs. The net result was that the Opposition parties were only given 13 places, although there were 32 Labour, Plaid Cymru and Liberal Democrat MPs all anxious to have a say about legislation that affected their localities, and in many cases, their constituency boundaries as well.

Such was the strength of opposition to the suspension of Standing Order 87 that all 32 Opposition MPs supported a Labour amendment opposing the Second Reading of the Bill because, amongst other defects, '... it fails to establish a directly elected all Wales tier of government.' As both the Shadow Secretary of State, Ron Davies, and Plaid Cymru's President, Dafydd Wigley, pointed out, this was the first occasion on which such an amendment had united all Opposition members representing Welsh constituencies against the Second Reading of a Bill relating exclusively to Wales. A measure of their outrage was indicated by one of Labour's Welsh Affairs spokesmen, Rhodri Morgan:

> The nature of the United Kingdom is at stake tonight. The UK is not one homogeneous nation state compris-

> ing 651 Members of Parliament who all represent the same sort of constituency. As its name shows the United Kingdom is amalgam of four different home countries ... The UK works because there is protection for the smaller parts — Scotland and Wales — to prevent them from being abused and pushed around by the much larger majority, England, when legislation goes through the House... The Government are trying to turn the Standing Committee into another Quango and pack it with Tory placemen in exactly the same way as they have done with all the Quangos.[3]

The significance of John Redwood, followed by William Hague, is that their origins as English MPs (for Wokingham and Richmond), compounded by their actions and demeanour in office as Secretaries of State for Wales, have served to dramatise for many Welsh people the points being made and largely unreported by Rhodri Morgan in the House of Commons in March 1994.

LABOUR'S RESPONSE AT WESTMINSTER

Labour's renewed commitment to an elected Assembly for Wales in the 1990s is a response to the underlying issues raised in such Parliamentary debates, together with the ever more blatantly partisan appointments to the Quangos. In the process the administration at the Welsh Office has come to be seen as not just an unrepresentative institution, but also autocratic and alien.

All Welsh Labour MPs have been radicalised to at least some extent by the uncongenial experience of a decade and more facing an increasingly arrogant and dismissive Welsh Office administration across the dispatch box at Westminster. The passage of the Welsh Language Bill through the House of Commons in the early 1990s was a case in point, particularly the response of MPs to the refusal of the Government to allow the Welsh language official status as part of the new Welsh Language Act. A reading of the debates during the summer of 1993 reveals an extraordinarily nationalist tone in the utterances of a wide cross-section of Welsh Labour MPs, a tone that would have been inconceivable in the 1970s. When, a year later, the government steamrollered its local government reorganisation legislation through Parliament the tone became even more shrill as MPs felt their personal constituency interests affected as well as a general principle.

These experiences account in large part for Labour's relative unity around the issue, in stark contrast to the party's divisions in the 1970s. At the same time another remarkable feature of Welsh devolution politics in the 1990s, compared with the 1970s, is the shift in position of the main protagonists inside the Welsh Labour Party. In the 1970s it was the leadership of the Welsh Executive and the Wales TUC that made the running. And it was Labour MPs in Parliament who brought change to a grinding halt, first by combining with other renegade Labour MPs from Scotland and Northern England to force a referendum, and then using it to defeat their party's official policy. In the 1990s these positions have been reversed. Now it is the party in Parliament that, with a few exceptions, that is trying to achieve as radical a consensus for change as possible. In contrast, the dominant voice on both the Welsh Labour Executive and inside the Wales TUC is for caution and hostile to any attempt at embracing progressive forces outside the Labour movement.

Why this shift has taken place reveals a good deal about the subterranean dynamics grinding away below the surface placidity of mid-1990s Welsh politics. In Parliament there has been a generational change within the Welsh Parliamentary Labour Party. As many as thirteen of the present twenty-seven Welsh Labour MPs have entered the Commons since 1979 and most are enthusiasts, albeit in varying degrees, for bringing the Welsh Office and the Quangos under the control of some kind of elected all-Wales body. Only three of the Labour MPs who have taken their seats since 1979 can be said to be lukewarm or hostile on the issue and two of those are inside the shadow administration. One of them, Kim Howells, MP for Pontypridd, actually had responsibility within the shadow Home Office team for co-ordinating devolution policy for the whole of the United Kingdom. The remaining two, Ray Powell (Ogmore), a whip, and Llew Smith (Blaenau Gwent) were hardly in the mainstream.

The Welsh MPs who campaigned most vigorously against devolution in the 1970s have all either left the Commons or recanted on the issue. In the 1979 referendum campaign an infamous, 'Gang of Six' MPs led the opposition. Since then, their leading figure Neil Kinnock has not only left for pastures new with the European Commission but actually declared his conversion in favour of an Assembly (at the first Welsh Grand Committee hearing in Cardiff in March 1993). Ifor Davies (Gower), Fred Evans (Caerphilly), and Ioan Evans (Aberdare) are all dead. Leo Abse (Pontypool) is retired.

The only one of the Six remaining in the Commons is Donald Anderson (Swansea East). But he announced his change of view during the run-up to the 1992 general election The centralising policies of the Thatcher government during the 1980s, he said, combined with the 'looming importance of the European dimension' had altered the terms of the argument:

> The heady nationalism of the 60s and 70s has spent its force. The case for decentralisation and democratic control on a UK basis is stronger. There is today the makings of a consensus on local government reorganisation. In any event devolution will elbow its way on to the stage of active political debate for there is the Scottish question ... A spectre is haunting our centralised structures, that of democratic accountability.[4]

THE POLITICS OF DEMOBILISATION

Why, however, has the Labour party leadership in Wales been endeavouring to keep the forces for change in check? If not actually back-pedalling it has certainly been trying to keep movement to a minimum. A first explanation is a fear of 1979 repeating itself. Those directly involved in the experience of the referendum of that year — and that includes many on the Welsh Executive — find it hard believe that things have really changed sufficiently to risk so soon a repeat of the angry debates, the divisions, and finally the rejection that the 1979 referendum brought about. Unlike Scotland, where there was a small majority in favour of the Scottish Assembly, in Wales there was a four-to-one rejection of the Welsh Assembly proposals. Hence the view that if there must be a policy then the less radical it is the better.

Linked to this feeling, especially among some of the larger trade unions, is the view that any controversial policy, and especially one as potentially fissile as devolution, is a dangerous diversion from the main project of returning a Labour government. During the 1970s the Wales TUC maintained a radical position insisting that a Welsh Assembly should have wide-ranging legislative competence and strong industrial powers. Now, however, it backed away from anything sounding like a fully-fledged Parliament, suggesting in December 1994 that 'a local government model has many attractions'. It was necessary to recognise, the Wales TUC continued, that

> Wales represents a small region within the UK in terms of population. It represents a peripheral region both within the UK and the European Union. As such Wales will need to continue to be a net recipient of regional transfers through the operation of regional policy and the tax and benefit system. As a net beneficiary of internal UK transfers, the Wales TUC does not think it appropriate for a Welsh Assembly to exercise powers over taxation or welfare benefits.[5]

This is a highly negative statement. It goes beyond the politics of demobilisation being discussed here and should be understood against the background of the Welsh culture of defeat that is analysed in Chapter 10. Even though the Conservatives are in office it is a paradox that while they, and the Wales CBI, continually 'talk up' the Welsh economy, Labour and the Wales TUC continually 'talk it down'. The reality in the mid-1990s is that the economy is extremely buoyant. During the past decade it has been experiencing what observers have described as a 'renaissance' based on large-scale inward investment and a surging renewal of manufacturing industry.[6] As described in Chapter 6, this has resulted in Welsh unemployment statistics lowering to the British average for the first time since the 1920s.

All this has not happened without a price. Inward investment has been attracted to a large extent because of relatively low wage rates. The improving employment statistics have hidden an underlying reality of a low domestic product per head, which in turn is a reflection of relatively low activity rates. What this means is that large numbers of people, especially older men, simply dropped out of the labour market once they were made redundant from the coal and steel industries in the 1980s. These groups, together with many thousands of young unemployed desperately need state intervention to bring them into the mainstream economy. In the Wales of the 1990s the British nation-state is patently failing such people. The radical response is to make a connection between democratic and economic renewal. Welsh political institutions are needed to defend the basic economic position of many thousands of people whose helpless plight is the by-product of success in the economy elsewhere. This is the case the Wales TUC should be making, rather than counselling the politics of demobilisation and defeat. A braver response is being provided elsewhere in the Labour movement, however, described in Chapter 5 which examines the role of the Shadow Secretary of State for Wales, Ron Davies.

In any event, the Wales TUC position ignores latest research suggesting that Wales is a net contributor to the British Exchequer. During 1994-5 the Treasury had a projected total gross income, by way of taxes and borrowing from Wales and from Brussels on account of Wales, of £12,586 million. Government projected spending in Wales for the same year, including pensions, social security payments, grants to local government and all other Central Government functions in Wales, amounted to a projected £12,555 million. Over the five years, 1990-95, Wales was calculated to have generated a £665 million surplus for the British Treasury.[7]

There is a further cautionary view, one partially linked to the others, and a curious blend of principle, sectarian pragmatism, and British nationalism. It was present in the 1970s and resurfaced once more, as the devolution issue returned with added prominence in the 1990s. This is the view that dismisses talk of devolution as parochial and small-minded when compared with 'real' issues like poverty in the Third World, anarchy in the currency market, problems with the ozone layer, or diminishing reserves of oil. It connects with a nervous rejection of 'narrow nationalism' and a feeling that it is global rather than Welsh politics that really matter or, at any rate, are safer and easier to manage. It is a perspective articulated most clearly by Pontypridd MP Kim Howells, who in this reflects the views of many on the Welsh executive, notably the GMB delegate Terry Thomas and the Rhondda secretary, Ken Hopkins, who chaired the party's policy commission examining constitutional change. As Howells put it, arguing the case against legislative powers for a Welsh Assembly:

> I think we've got enough government. I'm not somebody who believes in bigger government. I'm some-

> body who believes in smaller government, which sounds a bit strange, I suppose, coming from a member of the Labour Party.[8]

Underpinning this view, and made clear in the same interview, was a suspicion that 'lurking' behind even Labour's proposals was a nationalist agenda. In September 1995 he made the point on Scottish television, adding that he was worried about the potential 'Balkanisation of Britain', handing an easy target to the Scottish nationalists and creating anger and dismay amongst Scottish Labour Party leaders. The Shadow Home Secretary, Jack Straw, was forced to issue a statement saying that Howells' views did not represent party policy, and that as a devolution spokesman he had been 'out of order' in articulating them.[9] Nonetheless, they bear examination since they underpin much of the residual opposition to devolution in Labour's ranks. In the earlier interview, quoted above, Howells added that he was extremely cautious about constitutional change because Britain had not been overrun by the Nazis in the Second World War. Not only that, he said, unlike many other European countries, Britain had not elected fascists in the 1930s. The existing system had kept the 'extremists and nutters' out of Parliament, he continued:

> I've always been wary of nationalism. I'm probably the most anti-nationalist of all of the Labour group of MPs. I think that underneath nationalism always lurks fascism.

To equate nationalism with fascism, and especially during the Second World War, is a revealing a-historical reading of the period, as the Marxist historian Eric Hobsbawm — at one-time a fellow traveller on the Left with Kim Howells — has argued at some length. In his history of the twentieth century, *Age of Extremes*, he points out how, paradoxically, the fascism Kim Howells was referring to was essentially *internationalist*, with Germany seen as the core and only guarantee of a future European order:

> ... broadly speaking, whether a local nationalism found itself on the side of fascism depended on whether it had more to gain than to lose by the advance of the Axis.[10]

Kim Howells' resurrection of the *nationalist* question, though a throwback to the debates of the 1970s, and strangely out of tune with his own post-war generation, nonetheless still touches a raw nerve. For instance, it prompted the veteran Welsh nationalist leader, Gwynfor Evans, to offer the following reply in the form of a question: 'The two greatest nationalists of this century are Mahatma Ghandi and Nelson Mandela. Would Mr Howells tell us where he sees fascism lurking under the nationalism of these two great men?'[11]

A more convincing proponent of the same case, from the point of view of Kim Howells, would be Raymond Williams who, as early as 1967 (in his *Mayday Manifesto*), said the growing support for Scots and Welsh nationalism should be 'wholeheartedly welcomed'. Since Wales and Scotland had been politically and economically deprived by the existing system the national appeal in the two countries was, he said, inevitably radical:

> Nothing is more stupid than the stock response of some London-based Labour party people that nationalism of this kind is in some way ominous or that such descriptions as 'incipient fascism' can be used to characterise it. In real policies, what the nationalist parties are demanding is a necessary and inevitable challenge to a centralised managed politics and to a capitalism which, creating prosperity in favoured regions, creates poverty in unfavoured. The Scottish and Welsh nationalists are fortunate in being able to bring to these general protests that sense of a national identity which can quickly cross and dissolve existing political affiliations.[12]

Another way of exploring such contrasting interpretations of nationalism as actually experiencd in Wales, is to say that we are all nationalists, but whether that is regarded in a positive or negative light depends on the nationalism we are seen to support. In this argument, of course, Kim Howells is on the 'majority' British side, regarding Welsh nationalism as disruptive and backward looking. Raymond Williams' position in this debate was, as we shall see again in Chapter 8, that the British nation-state 'is at once too large and too small for the range of real social purpose'.[13] Speaking of those who regard the 'small nation' nationalism of the Irish, Scots, Bretons, Basques, or Welsh as especially backward, Williams added:

> It is sadly also true that not only the majority people, with 'their own' nation-state, but also many of the minority peoples, regard *this kind* of nationalism as disruptive and backward looking, and are even confident enough to urge 'internationalism' against it, as a superior political ideal. It is as if a really secure nationalism, already in possession of its nation-state, can fail to see itself as 'nationalist' at all.[14]

What is being described here is again, the politics of demobilisation which, with varying degress of intensity, has afflicted Welsh Labour as much as British Labour politics for much of the twentieth century. They are the politics of Labourism rather than socialism, a kind of nationalisation or incorporation of the radical impulses of democracy and socialism into a British safety standard of inactivism. Though, originally at least, Labour was a class-based party it has consistently failed to lead and defend its class at key moments, such as in the 1926 General Strike, and more recently in the 1984-5 miners' strike. The issue resurfaced once more during the summer of 1995 with attacks by marginalised elements on the left of the party on Tony Blair's style leadership. Always the priority of Labourism is to win votes, a priority that distances the party from its radical representative role.

That dilemma is compounded by involvement in the absorbing, co-opting, and ultimately disabling processes of Parliament. This is not something that just affects Labour. So far as Welsh politics are concerned it affects Plaid Cymru as well, which tends at key moments to back away from, for instnce dangerous questions around the Welsh language, often preferring to leave them to campaigning groups such as Cymdeithas yr Iaith.

The Westminster version of Parliamentary democracy is about power being handed down from above, rather than being exercised from below by the people, and so tends to blunted the radical edge brought to it by Labour and Plaid Cymru alike. It creates a contradictory position for both parties, but as far as the devolution question is concerned the impact on Labour is the most important. It compounds a political culture that is essentially demobilising, instinctively paternalistic, bred on patronage, and unused and unsympathetic to the democratic impulse. The kind of issues unleashed by devolution politics — the position of women, proportional representation, workers' control, and sustainable development as opposed to economic growth, to mention just four at random — are hardly music to its ears.

THE LABOUR DEBATE

All of which provided the backcloth to the Welsh Labour Party's annual conference in May 1995 where it had to decide the powers a Welsh Assembly should have and how it should be elected. Two years earlier the Executive had appointed a Constitutional Policy Commission to collect opinions on these and other questions. This was a gesture towards open politics, ostensibly the promotion of a wide-ranging debate and an opening of the party to views from outside. In practice, the six public hearings of the Commission held around Wales during the Autumn of 1994 were little advertised, low key afairs. They were held on weekdays rather than during the evenings or at weekends, times which minimised participation. Then Labour's Conference was presented with a document by the Commission to approve or reject. There was little room for amendments or debate.

By the time of the 1995 conference a few loose cannons had already fired off. Llew Smith, MP for Blaenau Gwent, had departed from an emerging consensus and called for a referendum. 'I did not join the Labour Party to follow the nationalist agenda,' he declared:

> For a future Labour government in its first year of office to be concentrating its attention on constitutional issues like an Assembly is in my opinion an insult to the unemployed, the homeless, those on low pay and the victims of crime.[15]

Llew Smith, however, was an isolated figure. His opposition to devolution was seen as at one with his even more ardent opposition to the European Union and all its works. In any event MPs and party activists at this stage were more concerned with presentation. What should an elected body for Wales be called? For some the term 'Assembly' suggested that it would be a 'talking shop'. For others, to call it a 'Parliament' aligned Labour too closely with Plaid Cymru.

In late 1994 Ron Davies, the Shadow Secretary of State, attempted to push the Liberal Democrat notion of a 'Senedd', as a middle way that could bridge the devolutionary spectrum. The idea, along with a suggestion that a Senedd would eventually have significant financial as well as legislative autonomy, was floated in a front page story in the *Western Mail* in November 1994, on the eve of a visit by Tony Blair to Cardiff. According to this report the Labour leader acknowledged the increasing popularity of the term 'Senedd' among Labour MPs and said,

> I'm perfectly happy with it personally, but I think what is more important is not what it is called but what the substance of the proposal amounts to.[16]

Ron Davies followed this up with an enthusiastic press notice the following day:

> Labour believes government should be accountable. 'Tony Blair has put himself and the Labour Party solidly behind a Senedd for Wales. We will direct money away from the Quangos and bureaucrats and to frontline services. We will save money wasted by Tory Quangos and placemen and put it under the Senedd's democratic scrutiny.

It was somewhat unfortunate, therefore, that a few days later a letter in the Western Mail, from Blair's Press Secretary Alistair Campbell, described the original story as misleading. 'The impression given of a substantial shift in policy is not borne out by the interview,' Campbell wrote. However, in a note beneath, the paper's political editor at the time, David Cornock, countered:

> Mr Blair offered the word *Senedd* in the knowledge that many MPs, including his Shadow Welsh Secretary, see this as a significant break with the 1992 Assembly policy.[17]

In the wake of this frisson, and under pressure from a number of Welsh MPs, most notably a sceptical Alan Williams (Swansea West), Ron Davies back-tracked to the term *Assembly*. It also became clear that while the Labour Policy Commission might open the way towards legislative competence, it would reject any notion of separate tax raising powers.

Challenged in the television studios on the apparent discrepancy emerging between Labour's policies for Wales and

Scotland, Ron Davies offered two explanations. Scotland, he said, was a different country with a different history and, most important of all, a different legal system which required its own legislative framework. There was a different scale of demand in Scotland which made tax raising powers more acceptable there. This led on to a second and more pragmatic justification. If at this stage Labour in Wales went down the road of tax raising, the debate over its plans would focus purely on that commitment and deflect attention from the main underlying democratic argument for devolution.

Left to themselves there was little doubt that Labour's key policy makers in Wales would have preferred to adopt a maximalist position on their emerging devolution scheme. However, they were reined back by more cautious elements and, in the process, found pragmatic arguments for doing so. The most controversial area proved to the method of election to the Assembly. Labour's consultative process uncovered a deep hostility to any electoral system other than first-past-the-post. 'Why should we hand over seats to the Tories or the Nationalists,' was a sentiment widely reflected in the views given the Policy Commission by the Wales TUC and some constituency parties.

Elsewhere in the party, and especially amongst those most in favour of devolution, there was an appreciation that Labour should not exploit its overwhelming electoral position. Instead, it was argued, Labour should adopt a self-consciously pluralist approach, which would be most clearly demonstrated by agreeing a system of proportional representation for elections to the Assembly.

The next critical moment occurred around the turn of 1994-5 when John Major, in a series of speeches and interviews, made it clear he would be placing Labour's devolution plans for Scotland, Wales and the English regions, at top of his agenda at the next general election. In a New Year message on BBC Radio 4 he declared that Labour's policies for England were 'teenage madness', while those for Wales and Scotland were 'one of the most dangerous propositions that has ever been put before the British nation'.

The effect was to throw Labour on to the defensive. A vigorous response was made by Labour's Front Bench spokesmen, for instance the Shadow Chancellor Gordon Brown at a press conference in Westminster the following week. However, the main impression was was that Tony Blair's advisers in London were only now seriously waking up to the devolution question, and seeing it in terms of a damage limitation exercise rather than a positive agenda for Labour.

Table 2: SUPPORT FOR WELSH DEVOLUTION

BBC Wales polls eliciting views on devolution were carried out during 1994, in March and October, and again in February 1995. The February 1995 poll, though commissioned from the same organisation, Beaufort Research, used a different data base, making comparisons between the three problematical. Taken together, however, they indicated a growing trend of support for an Assembly.

In the months leading up to the 1979 referendum which registered an overwhelming four to one opposition vote to the Assembly proposals of that time, the polls showed that people moved from a 'Don't Know' to a 'No' position. However, in the 1990s this trend may have been reversed. Two polls carried out by Mori in the first half of 1995 suggested that, answering the question whether they were in favour of "giving greater powers of government to Wales" respondents were moving from a 'Don't Know' to a positive position.

The BBC's March 1994 poll asked whether Wales should be "independent within the European Union". The February 1995 poll asked those "not opposed" to an Assembly — that is, those in favour and the Don't Knows —what kind they would prefer.

	FOR	AGAINST	DON'T KNOW
March 1994:			
Welsh Assembly	45 %	22 %	33 %
"Independence within the European Union"	37 %	36%	27 %
October 1994:			
Welsh Assembly	51 %	16%	33%
Feb 1995:			
Welsh Assembly	47 %	24%	29%

Of those "not opposed" in the Feb 1995 poll:

35% favoured an Assembly "Independent of Westminster, in Europe"
24% favoured an Assembly "Under Westminster, but with tax and law-making powers"
19 % favoured an Assembly "Under Westminster, but with limited powers"
3% favoured a "Consultative body only"
19% were "Don't knows"

MORI 1995 POLLS

To the question, are you in favour of "giving greater powers of government to Wales"

FEB 1995	60%	21%	19%
JUNE 1995	67%	23	10%

It was announced that a thorough review of Labour's policy for the English regions would be undertaken and a consultation paper issued. This duly appeared the following July, with the cautious stance adopted that is discussed in Chapter 8. At the same time the emerging policies for Scotland and Wales were put under the microscope. There was little that could be done about Scotland since irrevocable commitments — on law-making and tax raising powers and proportional representation — had already been made and published in the context of Labour's participation in the Scottish Convention. In Wales, however, the party's own Policy Commission was only then in the process of putting the final touches to its proposals, providing an opportunity for Blair's team to intervene.

A good deal of back-pedalling took place between meetings of the Commission held in January and February. Taxation powers for the Assembly had never been seriously on the agenda at this stage. However, there had been a prospect for primary legislative competence over the administrative functions exercised by the Welsh Office. Even more contentious, certainly so far as the presentation of Labour's policy was concerned, was the issue of proportional representation.

'SHAPING THE VISION'

When it eventually appeared, in May 1995, the Commission document *Shaping the Vision* fudged these questions. It reported that, 'Most respondents wished to see the Assembly having a defined legislative role'. Yet, it then went on to say that the Commission 'does not believe that the case has been established for general powers of primary legislation to be devolved to the Assembly'. It then conceded, with an obscurity of language that suggested it was being driven by an internal party debate:

> We recognise, however, that there may be a need for some specified powers to be devolved to enable the Assembly to discharge functions which have otherwise been devolved to it in relation to the restructuring of Quangos, the Welsh language and local government reorganisation.[18]

Did this mean that the Assembly was to have primary legislative powers in these three areas? What was certainly conceded was that the Assembly should have the power to debate and pass secondary legislation 'within the terms of primary legislation passed by Westminster, where the Act identifies matters of specific relevance to Wales.' Reading the document there is a sense that more than one hand was responsible for the final draft. A few paragraphs before the section on legislative competence just quoted, the document says that an Assembly is needed to help Labour deliver its policies 'for economic regeneration, for the health Service, and for education and training.' But it does not go on to explain how, without primary legislative powers, this is to be achieved.

For instance, there have been calls from the Welsh business community for an improved Welsh secondary system of education — for a Welsh baccalaureate modelled in part on what has been achieved by the separate Scottish secondary level system of education.[19] How would such a distinctive Welsh education system be put in place without primary legislation? The same applies to the economy, the health service and the rest of the domestic policy concerns for which an Assembly would be responsible.

Another defining question — put amongst others by the Plaid Cymru president Dafydd Wigley — is whether Labour's proposed Assembly would have been forced to implement the poll tax. This is cited in *Shaping the Vision* as a key example of the way measures have been imposed on Wales by the Conservatives against the wishes of the Welsh electorate. Yet without primary legislative powers it is difficult to see how an Assembly could have avoided the poll tax. The central government would simply have framed the primary legislation in such a way that it could not have been changed by secondary measures.

One reason Labour's policy makers are hesitating on the brink of a primary legislative role for the Assembly is because of the implications that would have for granting it tax determining powers as well. Such powers have been granted to Labour's proposed Scottish Parliament — a discretion to raise or lower the Scottish income tax by 3p in the pound. The requirement that elected institutions should have fiscal accountability built into them has been powerfully made by the Labour Party on more than one occasion in recent years. So, for instance, in the Policy Review document *Meet the Challenge: Make the Change*, in June 1989, Labour was unequivocal, though again the point related to Scotland:

> The priority is to make sure the financial powers are effective and allow real room for discretion. If Scotland's elected representatives want higher public investment they must raise the cash and answer for what they do at the ballot box. It is an essential discipline for any democratic arm of government.

In Wales, however, Labour appears fearful that pro-devolutionary sentiment is not strong enough to withstand the Conservative assault that its plans will be costly and result in greater taxation. Labour's hesitancy on taxation also reflects the deep-seated insecurity, discussed above in relation to the Wales TUC, that Wales has a relationship of economic dependency with the rest of the United Kingdom. One of the advantages of the latest phase in this long-running 'dependency' debate is that it promises to put an objective spotlight on Wales' income and expenditure statistics. The truth that is likely to emerge is that the Welsh budget is broadly in balance — certainly no less so than the UK as a whole — and likely to improve as the economy further diversifies and inward investment continues.

In any event, the question of dependency lays a false trail. Any serious proposals for devolution emanating from Westminster will have as an essential component a maintenance of the union of the United Kingdom. In these circumstances no central UK government, whether Conservative or Labour, will impose a tax settlement likely to provoke a nationalist response. These same arguments were heard over the creation of the Welsh Office in the 1950s. Who would now argue that the political muscle exerted as a result of the existence of the Welsh Office, whether under the Conservatives or Labour, has not been financially advantageous for Wales?

Yet criticism of the proposals outlined in the *Shaping the Vision* document, should not ignore the fact that they represent an important advance on the Assembly proposals contained in the 1978 Wales Act. There are two main reasons. First, a central thrust of the 1970s policy involved a separation of social and economic policy making in Wales. The Assembly then proposed would have had its main responsibility in social policy areas such as education, health and housing. Though control of the Welsh Development Agency was eventually conceded, following much negotiation between the Wales Labour Party and the Labour

Government of the time, the main responsibility for economic policy was left in the hands of the Secretary of State for Wales.

There is no such ambivalence in Labour's present *Shaping the Vision* document. It makes clear that an Assembly 'should take responsibility for the existing budget of the Welsh Office and its responsibilities' which include industry and economic development. The reluctance to concede as much in the 1970s was borne out of worries about the integrity of UK-wide economic policy making, and an anxiety to ensure a continued role for the Secretary of State for Wales. *Shaping the Vision* is merely a declaration about his position saying that he should continue in the British Cabinet and 'play an active part in discussions relating to all non-devolved matters'. It is not at all clear, however, how important these will be.

Labour's plans are an advance on the 1970s proposals for a second substantial reason: quite simply because during the 1980s and 1990s the powers, functions and finances of the Welsh Office have increased so much under the Conservatives. In the 1970s the Welsh Office had no discretionary power over its Treasury funding. Now it has a block of money and the Secretary of State for Wales allocates spending within it according to his own priorities. In the 1970s the Welsh Office capability for directing Welsh industry was extremely limited. Now it sets aims and objectives for the Welsh Development Agency, Welsh Development International, the Development Board for Rural Wales, Strategic Development policies such as the Valleys Project, and a raft of investment, technology and training initiatives.

Education and training have seen an enormous administrative expansion. In the 1970s there were no Training and Education Councils and there was a controversy over whether or not the Assembly proposed at the time should have responsibility for the University of Wales. Now the University already comes under the newly created Quango, the Higher Education Funding Council for Wales. In the 1970s there was no Curriculum Council for Wales, no Welsh Language Board, no Welsh Fourth Channel Authority, no Countryside Council for Wales, no Tai Cymru/ Housing for Wales, no Cardiff Bay Development Corporation, and the Arts Council of Wales was a sub-committee of the Arts Council of Great Britain. In the 1970s there were forty all-Wales Quangos. Today there are more than a hundred.

Labour's Assembly proposals entail giving elected representatives democratic control over the whole of this apparatus which was spending some £6.5 billion in the 1995-6 financial year.

UNFINISHED BUSINESS

One baseline requirement for Labour's policy is missing, however, and that is a sense of an across-Wales consensus. The *Shaping the Vision* document acknowledges that it was in the area of elections to its proposed Assembly that opinion was most divided amongst those who responded to the consultation: 'views were evenly split between those who favoured the retention of the existing first-past-the-post method of election and those who opted for a system which would reflect more accurately the proportion of votes cast.' The Commission itself offered two possibilities:

> (i) A first-past-the-post scheme with eighty members elected, two each from the forty Westminster constituencies.
> (ii) An additional member system, with eighty members elected on a first-past-the-post basis as in (i) above, with a further twenty members (four each from the five Welsh Euro-constituencies) 'allocated on a proportionate basis according to party preference expressed by voters, and consisting of losing candidates with the highest share of the vote in the relevant Westminster constituencies'.

The Welsh Executive responded by voting overwhelmingly for the first-past-the-post option, and this was pushed through the 1995 conference with little debate. Yet, as we shall see in Chapter 10, this remains a critical issue for Labour's policy, and one that most clearly reflects the contradictions in the party's approach. Once an Assembly is established we can be sure that greater legislative and taxation powers will accrue to it. This is the inherent nature of devolution which is a gradual process of change rather than a revolutionary event.

The political process of elections to the Assembly is a qualitatively different matter, however. Electoral systems are less susceptible to evolutionary change because they build in an immobilising self-interest of existing members from the start. They are also bound up with democratic acceptance and authority. The importance of the latter should not be underestimated, especially in a state like the United Kingdom which has no written constitution. The United Kingdom, with its antiquated notion of the indivisible sovereignty of 'Crown in Parliament', has no constitutional means whereby entrenchment of powers can be devised for local, regional or, in the case of Wales and Scotland, national Assemblies.

It was encouraging, therefore, to see that in the wake of the publication of Labour's plans a new pressure group was formed within party to campaign for a more radical approach. Welsh Labour Action was launched to secure for a Welsh Assembly:

* legislative and taxation powers
* a fair voting system
* equal representation for women
* direct representation of the Assembly in the European Union institutions

As Welsh Labour Action's chairman, Gareth Hughes, who was himself a member of the Labour Policy Commission, declared:

> By asserting that 'it does not believe that the case has been made for general powers of primary legislation to be devolved to the Assembly' the Commission is saying that the Palace of Westminster knows best and the people of Wales through its Assembly will be bit-part players allowed only to fill in the minor detail. Under the proposals a future Tory government would still be left unchallenged The document does not give any reasons for its view. Why it should arrive at this conclusion is even more intriguing when the report acknowledges that 'most respondents wished to see the Assembly have a defined legislative role'.
>
> The only conclusion that can be drawn is that as Labour edges toward power the old centralising urges of corporate Labourism are asserting themselves, allowing the wishes of the ordinary Welsh party member to be ignored on the assumption that the traditional loyalty to Labour in Wales can be taken for granted.[20]

The launch of Welsh Labour Action prompted a knee-jerk reaction from the Welsh Executive. Anita Gale, its general secretary, said the party's policy had been decided at the May conference:

> We would expect party members to adhere to this pol-

> icy. The process of amending this policy is over now. The time for amendment was during the past three years.[21]

However, soon after its launch Welsh Labour Action won the backing of a growing number of constituency parties, trade unions and figures such as Rhodri Morgan MP and MEPs Eluned Morgan and David Morris. The key unresolved issue remained proportional representation. In one extraordinary intervention, the chair of the Policy Commission, Ken Hopkins, attempted to argue that first-past-the-post could deliver a proportional result in elections to the Assembly.[22] What was being brought into play in these exchanges was a confrontation with the traditional Labourist politics of demobilisation. The outcome is far from certain, but the fact that a confrontation is taking place at all signals an important shift in Welsh politics.

It will be ironic if, in its eagerness not to be too far ahead of public opinion, Labour's policy makers fall too far behind. Opinion poll evidence suggests that those in favour of devolution tend to support a maximalist approach. Thus, in a February 1995 poll, shown in Table 2: (page 32) of the 76 per cent 'not opposed' to an Assembly (made up of 47 per cent in favour and 29 per cent Don't Knows) 35 per cent favoured an Assembly 'independent of Westminster, in Europe'; and another 24 per cent an Assembly 'under Westminster, but with tax and law-making powers'. Only 19 per cent favoured an Assembly 'Under Westminster, but with limited powers', the closest to Labour's policy as outlined in the *Shaping the Vision* document.

There are signs that a younger, more radical and less sectarian generation is emerging in Labour's Welsh constituency parties, a generation that reflects the politics that Tony Blair's leadership, on an optimistic reading, is offering. This is a politics committed to democracy from below rather than paternalism from above. However, the new generation have yet to achieve key positions on sufficient a scale to ensure their views are taken on board, especially where Welsh devolution is concerned. The danger for Labour is that it could saddle itself with a policy that will look dated, half-hearted and so difficult to campaign for in the critical years that lie ahead.

NOTES

1. *Western Mail,* 13 October 1994. The report 'Redwood warns on EU poor deal' quoted him as saying the European Community did not issue documents from Brussels in Welsh and was a linguistic centraliser, unlike national governments which had promoted 'regional languages'. This drew a sharp retort from Plaid Cymru president Dafydd Wigley. 'We can't speak Welsh at Westminster,' he said.
2. Peter Walker, *Staying Power: An Autobiography* (London: 1991) p.212.
3. Hansard, 16 March 1994.
4. Donald Anderson, 'Why I changed my mind on devolution', *Western Mail* 27 January 1992.
5. The Response of the Wales TUC to the Labour Party Consultation document *Shaping the Vision* (12 December 1995, Transport House, 1 Cathedral Road, Cardiff).
6. See, for example, Philip Cooke, Kevin Morgan, and Adam Price, *The Welsh Renaissance: Inward Investment and Industrial Innovation* (Centre for Advanced Studies in the Social Sciences, University of Wales College of Cardiff, 1994).
7. *Wales Still Paying it's Way!* (Plaid Cymru, 51 Cathedral Road, Cardiff, 25 November 1994). See also Dafydd Wigley MP, 'Defeating opponents scare tactics requires precision' in *Welsh Democracy Review*, Issue No 1, Summer 1995 (Parliament for Wales Campaign, 11 Gordon Road, Roath, Cardiff). Another analysis of Wales' accounts is given in Stephen Hill and Jon Owen Jones MP 'Calling the Tune: Funding a Welsh Parliament', in John Osmond (ed.) *A Parliament for Wales* (Llandysul: Gomer, 1994).
8. *Western Mail,* 11 May 1995.
9. *Glasgow Herald,* 'Howells "out of order" on devolution', 13 September 1995. Filmed in his constituency by BBC Scotland in August 1995, Kim Howells probably had little inkling of the controversy he would provoke. The timing, however, proved crucial. His interview was transmitted a few weeks later in the immediate aftermath of Scottish Labour's compromise with the Liberal Democrats over the number of MSPs the Scottish Parliament would have (129) and the way they would be elected — 73 by first-past-the post, topped up with 56 by PR from an additional member list. The same day as the Howells broadcast (on 11 September) Labour's Shadow Secretary of State for Scotland, George Robertson, had penned a statesmanlike article in *The Scotsman* saying this was only the beginning of change. 'No longer do issues like education, training and the arts have to live in sealed boxes administered by unelected boards and bossed by anonymous civil servants and unpopular ministers,' he wrote. 'We will create a new atmosphere of economic growth.'

Imagine Robertson's horror, therefore, when that very evening he saw Labour's man responsible for co-ordinating devolution for England, Scotland and Wales, saying he didn't regard it as a central issue: 'In seven years of campaigning, I have been asked about it two or three times on the doorstep, whereas I have faced two or three hundred questions on education and unemployment,' Kim Howells said. Yet the whole point for George Robertson was that devolution is urgently needed precisely to tackle issues like education and unemployment. The same case was being made by the Shadow Secretary of State for Wales, Ron Davies, who not long afterwards launched a new policy document, 'The Economic Case for a Welsh Assembly'.

This episode marked a dividing line between those, like Kim Howells, who continued to debate devolution using 1970s nationalist language, and those who saw devolution in 1990s European economic terms. Another great change from the 1970s was the way the unfortunate Kim Howells was handled in the aftermath of the debacle. Twenty years previously his political forbears — like Neil Kinnock, Leo Abse and Tam Dalyell — were allowed by the Labour leadership to get on with their wrecking opposition unimpeded. Kim Howells, however, was carpeted. Given the choice between resignation or the humiliation of a public rebuke, Kim Howells chose the latter. The episode shone a spotlight on Labour's commitment, refined and hardened it, and announced as publicly as could be that in the 1990s devolution — to deploy a Tony Blair expression — had moved on by a quantum leap since the 1970s.

10. Eric Hobsbawm, *Age of Extremes: The Short Twentieth Century* (London: Michael Joseph, 1994) p.136.

11. *Western Mail*, 16 May 1995.

12. Raymond Williams (ed) *Mayday Manifesto* (Harmondsworth: Penguin, 1968) pp.168-9.

13. Raymond Williams, *Towards 2000* (London: Chatto & Windus, 1983) p.197.

14. *Ibid.* p.183.

15. *Western Mail*, 14 December 1994. In January 1995 Llew Smith issued a 16-page personal manifesto, *The Welsh Assembly: Why it Has No Place in Wales*. This concluded: 'I strongly believe it is wrong to assume that institutional changes are the answer when our most urgent task is to develop a Labour movement capable of introducing socialist ideas relevant to our communities. Nationalism and all its ugliness can then be defeated by ideas, by alternative ideas that will excite people and provide them with a more decent and dignified life and courage to put them into practice. Pandering to the separatist aspirations of the Nationalists will not succeed. It will only debase our ideas, destroying all this is fine and unique in the Labour movement.'

16. *Western Mail*, 18 November 1994.

17. *Western Mail*, 22 November 1994.

18. *Shaping the Vision* (Wales Labour Party, 1 Cathedral Road, Cardiff, May 1995).

19. *Welsh Agenda*, Issue 2, April 1995 (Institute of Welsh Affairs, Ty Oldfield, Llantrisant Road, Cardiff) p.32. See also *Welsh Agenda*, Issue 3, Summer 1995, which carried an article by Professor David Reynolds on the issues involved. In the Autumn of 1995 the Institute of Welsh Affairs published a report on the potential for a Welsh Baccalaureate by Colin

Jenkins, of Atlantic College, and John David, Headmaster of Radyr Comprehensive.
20. Gareth Hughes, 'Re-Shaping the Vision' in *Red Kite* No 39, July/August 1995.
21. *Western Mail*, 10 August, 1995.
22. *Western Mail*, 24 August 1995. In this statement, contained in a Letter to the Editor, Hopkins suggested that with first-past-the-post and on the basis of the 1992 general election vote in Wales, an 80-member Assembly would produce 40 Labour seats and 23 or 24 for the Conservatives. The balance, he said, would be shared between the Liberal Democrats and Plaid Cymru, with the Liberal Democrats securing the higher number. Yet at the general election, of the 38 Welsh Parliamentary constituencies, Labour won 27 (with 49.5 per cent of the vote), Conservatives 6 (with 28.6 per cent), Liberal Democrats 1 (with 12.4 per cent) and Plaid Cymru 4 (with 9 per cent). On Hopkins' reckoning Labour should have won 19 seats, Conservatives 13 or 14, Liberal Democrats 3 or 4, and Plaid Cymru 2. That, however, would have been a proportional result.

LIVING IN QUANGOLAND

According to the Government, the number of Quangos in Wales has doubled to eighty since they took office in 1979. However, what constitutes a Quango is a controversial matter. If you add in bodies working at the local level and a swathe of advisory committees and tribunals — all of which 'fulfil a public purpose, are financed by public expenditure and are controlled by appointees' — then the Council of Welsh Districts has counted 350.[1] The main executive Quangos — those that spend significant amounts of money implementing government policies — are listed in Table 1 (page 45). During the 1993-4 financial year they were responsible for spending in the region of £2.5 billion. The bulk of this spending came out of the Welsh Office budget, comprising 34 per cent of the total. The entire revenue budget for Welsh local authorities was about the same, at £2.5 billion.[2]

The Secretary of State for Wales makes some 1,400 appointments to Welsh Quangos which employ around 60,000 people. Once the reorganisation of local government comes into force, after April 1996, there will be fewer elected councillors than people appointed to the Quangos — 1,273 serving on the 22 new authorities compared with 1,974 on the eight counties and 37 districts.

The Welsh Office and its Quangos constitute a formidable system of power, influence and patronage, a system which since 1979 has been controlled by a minority political party within Wales. The Welsh Office has a list of some 2,000 names of people who have been put forward — or who have put themselves forward — for public appointment. About 400 Quango vacancies are filled each year. When questioned on this subject by the Welsh Affairs Select Committee in December 1992 the former Secretary of State for Wales, David Hunt, said he would be happier with a more extensive list of up to 4,000 names. While agreeing that the most transparent system of making appointments was through public advertisement, he said he was 'very much in the hands of those locally who know individuals and know their calibre'.[3]

A rare insight into the way key appointments are sometimes

made was revealed by the chairman of the Wales Tourist Board, the former Glamorgan cricketer Tony Lewis, during the Welsh Select Committee's hearings. Interrogated by the Committee's chairman, Gareth Wardell MP, he described how he had been called to see the Minister of State at the Welsh Office, Sir Wyn Roberts, for an informal chat:

> We talked for a long time and he asked if I would consider public service, doing a job for Wales ... Then two months later he indicated, 'Would you accept tourism?' and I said, 'Yes'.
>
> *But in fact, no situation where you were asked detailed questions by a panel of people, nothing like that?*
>
> No.
>
> *Just a straightforward telephone call asking whether you would like the job and then a letter confirming your appointment?*
>
> Yes.[4]

A comprehensive survey of the membership of Welsh Quangos has been undertaken by David Hanson, Labour MP for Delyn. In December 1993 he published a survey of 452 appointees to 51 executive Welsh Quangos. Among the appointees were: 10 Deputy Lieutenants, 8 High Sheriffs, 14 OBEs, 9 MBEs, 15 CBEs, 7 Knights, 5 Honourables, 2 Peers, one Brigadier, one Major, one Lady in Waiting to the Princess Royal, and a wife of a former Cardiff Conservative MP. David Hanson concluded that the Quangos were 'overstuffed with white, male businessmen, lawyers and accountants, with a sprinkling of establishment figures for good measure. The pattern of appointments represents the face of the Conservative Party and their sympathisers, not the people of Wales'.[5]

THE NETWORK OF INFLUENCE

It is not just a question of appointments having a political edge, but the way the same personalities keep cropping up time and again. Between them they are creating an intermeshed network of influence. Examples of the way key appointees are responsible for more than one powerful body, and also often have strong Conservative Party links, are given in table 2 (page 47).

Table 1: MAIN EXECUTIVE QUANGOS

ECONOMIC DEVELOPMENT / ENVIRONMENT / HOUSING	Annual expenditure*
Welsh Development Agency	£78m
Development Board for Rural Wales	£16m
7 Training and Enterprise Councils	£120m (approx.)
Cardiff Bay Development Corporation	£47m
Wales Tourist Board	£15.7m
Land Authority for Wales	self-financing
Countryside Council for Wales	£17m
Tai Cymru/Housing for Wales	£185m
HEALTH	
9 District Health Authorities	£1, 274m
8 Family Health Service Authorities	£462m
Health Promotion Authority for Wales	£4m
Welsh Health Common Service Authority	£50m
EDUCATION AND CULTURE	
Higher Education Funding Council	£232.5m (1994-5)
Further Education Funding Council	£160m (1994-5)
Curriculum Council for Wales	£1.5 m
Arts Council of Wales	£13m
CADW (Welsh Historic Monuments)	£15m
Sports Council for Wales	£6m
Welsh Language Board	£1.9m (1994-5)
Wales Youth Agency	£0.4m
Broadcasting Council for Wales	£61m
S4C (Welsh Fourth Channel Authority)	£58.5m

* Funding figures are for the year 1992-3. Where a Quango has recently been created, funding is given for 1994-5

The network of influence is not confined to multiple chairmanships and overlapping membership of Quangos. Many leading Quango figures also run key cultural institutions in Wales. The membership of the Board of the Welsh National Opera and the Council of the National Museum is a useful beginning for a gazetteer. During 1992-3, for example, the chairman of the National Museum's Council was Timothy Edwards, brother of Lord Crickhowell, the former Secretary of State for Wales who by this time was chairman of the National Rivers Authority, chairman of the Cardiff Bay Arts Trust and also a member of the Board of the Welsh National Opera. The deputy chairman of the Museum's Council was Mathew Prichard, a cousin of Lord Crickhowell. At the time Prichard was also chairman of the Arts Council of Wales. Such connections allowed Rhodri Morgan, MP for Cardiff West, to observe:

> Lord Rothschild said that the good chap theory of government in England was based on picking people who were 53, white, male, residents of the south-east of England and members of the Reform club ... If applied to Wales the theory would be based on picking people who were white, male, resident in the south-east of Wales, owning a farm in the Vale of Usk, being frequent dinner guests of Lord and Lady Crickhowell and possibly supporters of the Welsh National Opera.[6]

The record of Lord Crickhowell (Nicholas Edwards) is especially instructive. As Secretary of State for Wales he was one of the main instigators of the Cardiff Bay Development project. In 1988, after leaving office, he joined the board of Associated British Ports (ABP). A year later two valuable parcels of ABP's land within Cardiff Bay — 160 acres worth an estimated £50m — were excluded from compulsory purchase by the Cardiff Bay Development Corporation. On one of the sites, a 100 acres at Roath Basin, Grosvenor Waterside a subsidiary of ABP, constructed a prestigious office block, known as Crickhowell House. This was rented to the Welsh Health Common Services Authority (another Quango) at £14 per square foot — a sum at the top end of office rents in central Cardiff, let alone the area of Cardiff Bay. What was the reason for the land being excluded from compulsory purchase? Was this an example of the network of influence at work? In the House of Commons in February 1995 Rhodri Morgan described the sequence of events as 'an example of government sleaze of the kind with which we have become all too familiar'.[7]

Lord Crickhowell's permanent secretary when he was at the Welsh office was Sir Richard Lloyd Jones. Not long after his retirement he was made chairman of the Welsh Arts Council, in succession to Matthew Pritchard, in 1994. The remuneration for this post is nil. Not long afterwards, however, he was made chairman of the newly created Quango, the Staff Commission for Wales whose job is to safeguard employees' interests during the local government reorganisation: remuneration for this post is £15,900 a year for an average 1.5 days-a-week work.

The way Quangos often operate was exemplified by the Higher Education Funding Council when it intervened in a long-running dispute between the colleges of the University of Wales over its federal status. In the early 1990s they reached a compromise which preserved their identity but also allowed them access to the services of the University's central registry in Cardiff. However, this arrangement was undermined by the Funding Council in favour of a market-orientated subscription-based funding system. According to the University's Vice-Chancellor at the time, Professor Kenneth O. Morgan, this meant the colleges could only use the registry haphazardly. He accused the Funding Council of 'an aggressive and interventionist approach' that threatened the integrity of the University of Wales, adding:

> There is immense discontent at the operation of a series of Tory-led Quangos covertly undermining local government and other institutions in Wales.[8]

Table 2: QUANGOS: THE NETWORK OF INFLUENCE

David Rowe-Beddoe: chairman of the Welsh Development Agency and the Development Board for Rural Wales. Member of the Conservatives Abroad Strategy Committee at the 1992 election, and chairman of its Monaco branch.

Dr Gwyn Jones: chairman of the BBC Broadcasting Council for Wales, former chairman of Welsh Development Agency. Originally appointed as chairman of the Welsh Development Agency in 1987 after a chance meeting with the then Secretary of State for Wales, Peter Walker, at a Conservative fund-raising lunch.

Sir Idris Pearce: chairman of the Higher Education Funding Council for Wales; deputy chairman of the new Urban Regeneration Agency. Tory candidate for Neath in the 1959 general election.

Michael Griffith: chairman of the Countryside Council for Wales; member of the Higher Education Funding Council for Wales; chairman of the Glan Clwyd District General Hospital NHS Trust. Vice-Lord Lieutenant of Clwyd; once described himself as a 'crusty old Tory' (Western Mail, 25.11.92) .

Sir Geoffrey Inkin: chairman of the Cardiff Bay Development Corporation and the Land Authority for Wales. Tory candidate for Ebbw Vale in the 1979 general election; a runner-up for the Conservative nomination for Cardiff North in 1983.

Sir Donald Walters: chairman of the Llandough Hospital NHS Trust; member of the Development Board for Rural Wales; until 1993 deputy chairman of the Welsh Development Agency. President of the National Union of Conservative and Unionist Associations.

A VACUUM OF RESPONSIBILITY

The well-publicised problems at the Welsh Development Agency have probably done more than anything else to focus attention on the issue of the accountability of Quangos. The problem goes deeper than just the Quango system itself, however. Experience has exposed a vacuum of responsibility at the top of the Welsh government machine, with blame for wrong-doing being passed back and forth between the Welsh Office and the Quangos, in this case the Welsh Development Agency.

Among the irregularities at the WDA exposed by the House of Commons Public Accounts Committee during 1993 were questionable redundancy payments costing more than £1m; an abortive £308,000 attempt to privatise the agency, known as *Operation Wizard*; free private motoring for board members; and the appointment of a discharged bankrupt as head of marketing. It might be argued that in exposing these irregularities the Public Accounts Committee demonstrated the effectiveness of the House of Commons in holding Quangos to account. Yet such an examination of a particular organisation is a rare occurrence at Westminster and can only expose wrong-doing after the event. More fundamentally, however, the episode exposed a vacuum of responsibility at the core of Welsh administration. In a statement on the Public Accounts Committee report into the Welsh Development Agency John Redwood distanced the Welsh Office from involvement. He said that it was clear that: 'my predecessors were not to blame, and that the primary responsibility lay at executive level in the WDA'.[9]

There is no doubt, however, that the political motivation for *Operation Wizard* came directly from Peter Walker when he was Secretary of State for Wales in the late 1980s. Answering questions following his Commons statement, John Redwood also absolved the chairman of the Agency at the time, Dr Gwyn Jones, from responsibility. 'The former chairman is not held primarily to blame for those events,' he said.

Yet this is contradicted in an internal inquiry into the affairs of the WDA, conducted by the former Permanent Secretary at the Department of Education and Science, Sir John Caines. His report was lodged in the library at the House of Commons the same day John Redwood made his Commons statement. It contains repeated references to Dr Jones's role in *Operation Wizard*, saying 'he was closely involved from mid-1988.' More generally, the report adds, 'accountability must start at the top with the board'.[10] Dr Jones left his £40,610 a year, two-and-a-half days a week post in 1993 just ahead of publication of the Public Accounts Committee report. However, he remained chairman of the Broadcasting Council for Wales (remuneration, £15,140 a year) with a seat on the BBC's UK Board of Governors.

In this last position Dr Jones has also courted controversy. The outstanding instance was his notorious attempt to reprimand BBC Wales journalists who had investigated a Welsh Development Agency land deal in which he himself was involved, albeit indirectly. In May 1994 the BBC Wales' *Week In Week Out* current affairs programme undertook an investigation into the WDA's involvement with the Cynon Valley Borough Council in pursuing a land deal in Aberdare. According to the programme the WDA secretly favoured one developer over another, thereby breaking its own rules. Later the Welsh Affairs Select Committee in the House of Commons confirmed the story. It found that the Agency had bought the land for £440,000 from a company which had just days earlier paid only £160,0000 for it. The Committee said it appeared that Tesco, which later acquired the site, had been given preferential treatment.[11]

The Aberdare land deal took place while Dr Gwyn Jones was still chairman of the Welsh Development Agency. He also happened to be a director of Tesco at the time as well. A month after the *Week In Week Out* programme was broadcast, during a meeting of the Broadcasting Council he was chairing, Dr Jones attacked the investigation as 'unpatriotic and detrimental to Wales's economic interests'. Around the table were two other members of the Council who also had an interest in the issue: Tony Roberts, chief executive of the Cynon Valley Borough Council, and Enid Rowlands, then Director of Targed, the Gwynedd Training and Enterprise Council, but shortly to become North Wales Managing Director of the Welsh Development Agency.

Needless to say, BBC Wales management strongly resisted this attack and thereby reduced the damage done to BBC Wales' journalistic integrity. Even so the episode stands as an outstanding instance of the way in which the network of Quango influence can be manipulated.

THE ONWARD MARCH OF INSTITUTIONS

It is a key dimension of Quangoland that so much of it has been created by successive Conservative administrations at the Welsh Office since 1979. Of course, the Welsh Office has been in existence since 1964 and has grown steadily ever since. Founded with just 225 civil servants and a budget of less than £300m it now has around 2,300 civil servants and a budget of nearly £7 billion. The Welsh Office's running costs for 1994-5 were £63.387m.

Quangos did not begin their career with a Welsh Conservative government in 1979. The Welsh Development Agency and the Development Board for Rural Wales, for example, were set up under a Labour government in the mid-1970s as part of a gathering momentum towards political devolution. Yet despite the 1979 referendum the bureaucratic government machine at the Welsh level has continued to evolve. In the process government power in Wales has been taken far beyond what was envisaged in the 1978 Wales Act, in three main directions :

* There has been an extension in Welsh Office powers with it negotiating a block grant directly with the Treasury and then allowed discretion for its allocation between functions.

* More all-Wales institutions, many of them Quangos, have been created.

* There has been a growing European dimension to Welsh policy-making. Examples have been the establishment of a European Division within the Welsh Office, the establishment of a Wales office in Brussels, and the negotiation of bilateral trade and cultural agreements with the European 'Four Motor' regions — Baden-Wurttemberg, Catalunya, Rhones Alpes, and Lombardy.

The extension of the Welsh government machine in these directions has done a great deal to strengthen and promote Wales's separate identity and renewed demands for an elected Welsh Assembly or Parliament. Yet they have been carried through by a Conservative, Unionist government, ostensibly dedicated to maintaining the United Kingdom as a unitary State. There are a number of interlocking pressures behind this contradiction:

* The Welsh Office which the Conservatives inherited in 1979 presented a curious mix of both inertia and an instinct to accumulate more functions.

* In the hands of their political allies and sympathisers the Quangos offered the Conservatives a way of by-passing Labour and Independent-controlled local government.

* Wales provides a convenient administrative unit in terms of size, one that fits in well with the demand from Brussels that regional planning and action are a prerequisite for funding.

* A growing demand from the network of Welsh institutions themselves for co-ordination of administration at the all-Wales level — a demand that was conceded by the Conservatives during 1994 with the creation of the Welsh Economic Council.

This last is a kind of super-Quango made up of heads of other Quangos, like the WDA and the Higher Education Funding Council, together with representatives from the Wales CBI and Wales TUC. The aim, according to the Conservative's own Manifesto at the 1992 election was to 'ensure greater cohesion and a more united effort on the part of the Principality's major employers' and employees' organisations.' Yet, as the Labour MP for Neath, Peter Hain, remarked:

> While recognising the need for a strategic, all-Wales approach that was a recipe for corporatism, not democracy. Where are the people in all of this?[12]

NOTES

1. Council of Welsh Districts, *Quangos in Wales - A Discussion Document*, January 1995. Most of the expenditure figures in Table 1 are derived from this document.
2. The statistics quoted in these paragraphs can be found in: Kevin Morgan and Ellis Roberts, *The Democratic Deficit - A Guide to Quangoland*, Department of City and Regional Planning, University of Wales College of Cardiff, October 1993.
3. Welsh Affairs Committee, *The Work of the Welsh Office*, HMSO, 27 January 1993.
4. *Ibid.*
5. David Hanson MP, *Unelected, Unaccountable and Untenable - A study of appointments to public bodies in Wales*, December 1993.
6. Hansard, 26 May 1993.
7. See Chris Blackhurst, 'Top Tory accused of 'sleaze' over dockland land deals', *Independent on Sunday*, 5 February 1995.

8. David Cornock, 'Professor marks Quango poorly', *Western Mail*, 16 November 1994
9. Hansard, 19 October 1993.
10. John Caines, Clive Beck, J. Geraint Davies, *Inquiry into the findings of The Committee of Public Accounts concerning the 1991-2 accounts of the Welsh Development Agency*, House of Commons Library, 17 October 1993.
11. *Western Mail*, 18 July 1995.
12. Peter Hain, 'Empowering the People', in John Osmond (ed.) *A Parliament for Wales* (Llandysul: Gomer Press, 1994) p.274-5.

DEMOCRACY IN THE BALANCE

The 1990s local government reorganisation was aimed at improving Welsh democracy by making it simpler and easier to understand. This, at any rate, was the stated view of the Ministers who forced it through, against the opposition of all Welsh Labour, Plaid Cymru and Liberal Democrat MPs in the House of Commons. As Welsh Office Minister Gwilym Jones put it:

> The steps we are taking to reform local government will enhance local democracy, will improve links with central government and will continue the process of real devolution. By removing an entire tier of local government and reducing the number of principal councils in Wales from 45 (8 counties and 37 districts) to 22 we will reduce friction and dsuplication within local government, as well as improving value for money and accountability.[1]

Yet from the beginning it has been a clear intention of the Government that a wide variety of joint arrangements between the new authorities will emerge to ensure the delivery of key services, notably those formerly carried out by the eight counties. What is emerging in practice is a new two tier local government system. The difference is that instead of two tiers of democratically accountable government, one will be directly elected and the other indirectly elected, made up of a variety of joint arrangements, bodies and committees.

In every service area — except environmental health and waste collection — there is an expectation in the Local Government (Wales) Act 1994 that some joint arrangement will be required, particularly for strategic planning and the provision of specialist services. These arrangements will be voluntary in social services, housing, transport planning, highways, economic development, trading standards and leisure services. However, in four areas the Secretary of State has 'reserve powers' to encorce collaboration if suitable voluntary arrangements do not emerge — for education, public libraries, museums and galleries, and land use planning.

When the Welsh Office issued its first consultation paper on the changes, in June 1991, it emphasised the improvement in democratic accountability that the changes should bring.[2] As it emerged, however, the legislation stressed instead the perceived improvements in efficiency and cost-effectiveness the reorganisation would achieve. These, it was claimed, would result from the introduction of market forces into the delivery of public services. This is the main intention of Compulsory Competitive Tendering for much of local authority service provision, amongst the more complicated aspects of the reorganisation. Whether this approach will prove to be more efficient and cheaper, lead to greater understanding of local government by the public and, most questionable of all, improve democratic accountability, are all matters of doubt.

There is every likelihood that rather than cutting costs the new system will be inflationary. Approximately 66 per cent of local government spending under the old system was undertaken by the eight county councils (the figure was nearer 80 per cent if capital expenditure and spending financed by fees and rents are taken into account). Under the new system administration of this expenditure will be expanded to twenty-two new councils. Though Welsh Office directives constantly emphasise the need for joint arrangements and new methods of service delivery, the scope for increased administration and therefore increased costs is plain.

The view taken at the time of the last reorganisation of local government, during 1972-4, and also when elected local government was first created in the 1880s, was that as far as possible a level of government should be created for each level of service delivery. There was an assumption that a multi-tier process of service delivery requires a multi-tier structure of government.

Criticism of this approach is well rehearsed. The division of responsibility between tiers was never understood by the electorate, it was said. Further, it was believed that the separate accountability of service managers in the various tiers worked against effective co-operation, for example between housing (districts) and social services (counties).

On the basis of such arguments a consensus appeared to emerge in Wales in the 1970s and 1980s in favour of the unitary authority approach. However, the consensus broke down when it came to deciding what should be the optimum size of the unitary authorities to be created. On the one hand there were those — usually in existing county government — who argued that the single tier must operate a scale at least as large as the largest scale required for any aspect of service delivery. So, if strategic planning or specialist resource provision required a population of 500,000, then that should be the minimum scale for local government.

On the other hand there was an alternative view — most clearly associated with the districts, but also with the official policies of the Opposition political parties — that populations of 300,000 to 500,000 were too large to relate to long-established patterns of community identity.

The debate that ensued was clouded by the obvious self-interest on the part of the key participants, namely the thirty-seven districts and eight counties. Nonetheless, what was at stake was perhaps the key underlying, and untested, question so far as the present reorganisation is concerned: that is, the inevitable separation in many cases of the boundaries of the new so-called unitary authorities from the arenas in which actual service delivery will occur.

What this will mean in practice will be the introduction to local government on a large scale of the essentially commercial idea of separating the *purchaser* function from that of the *provider*. Of course, in itself the principle of this is not new to local government which is well-used to buying in some specialities and services. What is creating the new situation, however, is the scale on which the purchaser/provider split is likely to apply, a scale so far only previously experienced in the public sector with the National Health Service. That this project can be successfully accomplished has been the fundamental proposition of those behind the change. A Welsh Office paper *The Purchasing/Enabling Function*, dated June 1992, comments:

> Direct delivery of services is only one option among the whole range of mechanisms open to authorities for securing services and obtaining value for money. Increasingly, the emphasis is moving towards a mixture of direct and indirect provision requiring a clear distinction to be drawn between the functions of purchasing and providing ... (3)

THE MARKET VERSUS DEMOCRATIC ACCOUNTABILITY

The thrust of this approach is an attempt to inject more market and commercial considerations into the operation of local government, rather like the purchaser-provide split that has been introduced into the National Health Service. On the whole the approach was viewed positively by key policy makers from the existing district level of local government in Wales. For example, the Assistant Secretary of the Council of Welsh Districts, Paul Griffiths, welcomed the introduction of a purchaser/provide split into local government which, he said, would:

> ... replace management through bureaucratic hierarchy with the more challenging, and potentially more effective, management through delegation, contract, negotiation, partnership and collaboration.
>
> This will be the challenge for the future in Welsh local government. We need institutions for local government that are based on a community's sense of identity and common interest. We need local authority members and managers who can be effective and accountable without assuming hierarchical control over all necessary resources. If this is achieved we can look forward to an enhanced local democracy based on enhanced public understanding, control and support.[4]

It is noteworthy, however, that with the papers accompanying the Welsh Office note on *The Purchasing/Enabling Function* (quoted above) was placed another, *The Supplemental Note by the Chief Executives of the eight Welsh County Councils* This included the following observations which amounted to a fundamental attack on the legislation as it has now been enacted:

> It is already evident that, to secure the continuation of effective planning, provision and delivery of local services, a proliferation of joint arrangements will be required. The Consultative Council is asked to note that it has already been acknowledged ... that any joint arrangements relating to strategic planning and purchasing, which are short of being prescriptive, cannot be relied upon.
>
> The Secretary of State (in his first consultation paper, *The Structure of Local Government in Wales*, June 1991) identified five principles by which the reorganisation of local government should be judged:
>
> * Local authorities should be democratically accountable to their electorates.
>
> * Local public services should be responsive to the wishes, needs and circumstances of local communities.

> * The role of local authorities and their responsibilities for service delivery should be clearly understood by local people.
>
> * Local authority boundaries should, as far as possible, reflect and strengthen existing community loyalties.
>
> * Local public services should be of high quality and delivered efficiently, economically and effectively.
>
> District and county officers, with Welsh Office officials, have sought to identify the best possible arrangements for securing the provision of services based around twenty-three authorities (the number at that stage proposed). It is again evident, however, to the Chief Executives of the eight Counties, that the proposals emerging will *not* meet the five principles of the Secretary of State. The proliferation of joint arrangements will undermine democratic accountability, be administratively unwieldy, and be less understood by local people than at present. The emerging arrangements for both planning and delivery of services give serious cause for concern. They are unlikely to be robust. Neither do they meet the requirements for efficiency, economy and effectiveness ...

Two key areas where administration under the new system will be put to the test are education and social services where twenty-two authorities will in future be responsible for functions that were previously carried out by eight. What are the likely implications of this expansion?

EDUCATION

Strategic planning for education will be among the biggest problems facing the new unitary councils. The role of an Education Authority has changed significantly in recent years with the advent of Local Management of schools and the growth, albeit at a very slow rate in Wales, of grant-maintained schools that have 'opted out' of local authority control. Indeed, those responsible for the new system assumed that the responsibility of the Education Authority would be reduced even further in future. Why else whould they frame legislation that would not even require the new Councils to establish Education Committees?

Problems were highlighted very early on in the policy process, in August 1992, when three leading Directors of Education resigned from a Welsh Consultative Council Sub Group on Education. They were Eddie Roberts (Mid Glamorgan), John Beale (West Glamorgan), and Gwilym Humphrys (Gwynedd). In a signed statement, lodged with the Welsh Office papers, they declared:

> The Welsh Office officials will know of our reservations that, with the possible exception of two or three of the largest unitary authorities, the extent of joint working is such as to be near the limits of feasibility. To this already complex pattern of joint working, the White Paper (on Education, entitled *Choice and Diversity*) has added a further partner — the Schools Funding Council. Furthermore, the proposal to eliminate Education Committees will weaken the focus of strategic planning within the unitary authorities. Add to all this the uncertainty to be brought to planning and budgeting as schools opt out individually or in clusters for grant maintained status, and coherent planning becomes less and less likely.
>
> We believe that the establishment of many small unitary authorities, combined with the proposals in the White Paper, will introduce such confusion and instability into the planning of schools provision in Wales that we would not wish as professional education officers to be identified with such a state of affairs.

These were trenchant criticisms. However, they were not met with support from the district side in the argument. Their view was that joint arrangements of the kind being envisaged could be forward looking and successful. The essence would be co-operation, and out of that would come greater flexibility and maturity on the part of the organisatuions concerned. As one of the district participants put it:

> It is only inward looking, autocratic organisations that cannot share power a responsibility through partnertship relations.[5]

There is also the view that since most of the new councils will have a population exceeding 100,000 they will be able to avoid the more radical versions of the 'enabling authority' originally envisaged.[6] That is to say, most of their services will still be directly delivered by the councils themselves. However, in the two key service areas being considered here — education and social services — the specialisms and sub-regional planning needed are highly likely to require joint arrangements, or what more optimistically might be termed 'a new culture of partnership'.

Moreover, the clear intention of those who framed the legislation was to diminish the role of elected local government, especially in education. Thus the present Government foresees more and more schools opting out of local government control and eventually being funded directly by the projected Schools Funding Council for Wales. The financial inducements and pressure being exerted to persuade schools to opt out signals a determination to see the twenty-two new councils have a much reduced educational role.

The policy has not proved popular, even in hitherto Conservative strongholds. By mid-1995, after three yers of policy, only eleven of Wales's 227 secondary schools, and just five of the 1,704 primary schools had opted out. A test case came in late 1994 at the West Monmouth Secondary School where a second vote on opting out was insisted on by the Welsh Office following allegations that the first vote, registering 60 per cent of parents against, had not been properly conducted. The second vote, registered 70 per cent of the parents against opting out. An indication of the pressure on the Gwent Education Authority was given by Phil Rees, the School Governor who led the campaign in favour of opting out. 'With £9m education and staff cuts coming up in Gwent, we still believe Grant Maintained Status would have been the best option', he said.[7]

The reorganisation seems bound undermine the traditional educational role of local government. Many of the twenty-two new authorities will not be able to employ directly many of the specialist advisory services needed for the schools for which they are responsible. They will have to enter into purchasing agreements with other authorities (under Section 25 of the 1994 Act), or Agency agreements with another authorities (under Section 10 of the Act). Alternatively they could establish a local authority company to supply educational advisory services.

All twenty-two unitary authorities will undoubtedly want to establish education committees and an education department with at least a chief education officer. At the same time it is likely that joint committees between authorities will allocate key strategic education functions to one authority amongst their number. It will be less than surprising if the areas covered by these committees turn out to correspond with the present county boundaries.

SOCIAL SERVICES

Devising delivery mechanisms for social services is probably the most demanding of all the functions of local government. Social services are unique in their variety, complexity and public sensitivity and, moreover, interact intimately with other services such as housing and the NHS.

From the start there was a divergence of view between the policy makers on how social services should be organised. The Assembly of Welsh Counties remained firmly of the view that nothing less than statutory joint arrangements between groups of the new unitary authorities could ensure continuity in management and planning. Yet a presumption of the Government, carried through in the legislation, was that in this field of administration and policy statutory joint boards should be avoided.

Instead, the Government's position has been that the new authorities should move towards being enablers and purchasers of social service functions. This would allow the injection of the private sector and market forces into a key area of local government. At the same time it is recognised that social services have a special sensitivity and that accountability must remain clear and unencumbered. Hence the 1994 Local Government (Wales) Act insists that this is the only functional area where the new councils must establish an appropriate committee.

Under the new system the Council social services departments will work increasingly closely with the NHS. This will have particular implications for the Care in the Community service where there are now numerous grey areas of operation between the social service responsibilities of local councils and the medical responsibilities of the Health Service.

The NHS in Wales is itself being reorganised and its own new structure comes into effect in April 1996, at the same time as the local government reorganisation. Wales will then have five health authorities instead of seventeen. This reorganisation will also involve the merger of district health authorities and family health service authorities. The boundaries the five new Health Authorities deliberately coincide with those of combinations of the new unitary authorities, as follows:

> North Wales — combining Gwynedd and Clwyd.
>
> Mid Wales — combining Powys and Dyfed.
>
> West Glamorgan — plus the new unitary authority area of Bridgend.
>
> Gwent — plus the new unitary authority area of Caerphilly.
>
> South and Mid Glamorgan — that is the new unitary authority areas of Cardiff and the Vale together with Rhondda, Cynon, Taff and Merthyr.

A likely option is for strategic management of social services to evolve on the basis of these five sub-regions of Wales. This would entail collaboration between the councils in each area. Two possible models of future administration will then be evident:

> (i) Pressure for the Health Authorities to take over the councils' social services function.
>
> (ii) Pressure for the councils to take on the Health Authority function by taking over its health commissioning role.[8]

The 'purchaser-provider' split is already an essential part of the NHS and is steadily informing the culture of local government-provided services, a process that will be accelerated by the reorganisation. As a management tool the 'purchaser-provider' split is a neutral concept. The questions are: who does the planning and purchasing and to what extent are they accountable to the public they serve?

THE THREAT TO DEMOCRACY

It is plain from this brief discussion that direct provision of education and social social services by the twenty-two new councils

— two of their most important functions — is likely to be eroded. They will be unitary only in the sense of having oversight responsibility for ensuring the delivery of local services. In many cases they will be reduced to overseeing often complex joint arrangements in which they will purchase the services of staff working for other authoities or private concerns.

Will democracy be in the balance under this new system? The intention to create an indirectly elected second tier of joint arrangements between authorities is one strong indication that it will. Another is the absence of an all-Wales tier of directly elected government.

The growth in the number and influence of the Quangos since the 1970s has been to a large extent at the expense of elected local government. The thirty-seven Welsh district councils have lost most of their housing responsibilities to Tai Cymru/Housing for Wales, although the management of more than 200,000 council houses still remains an important local government function. The eight County Councils have lost control of further education to the Further Education Funding Council for Wales. It is the clear intention of the present administration to establish a Schools Funding Council for Wales if sufficient schools decide to opt out.

Quangos do not operate only at the all-Wales level. There are now a whole range of government functions carried out below the all-Wales level by bodies other than elected local councils. These are essentially local Quangos. Many are responsible for functions previously handled by elected councils, functions over which the councils have some duty of care and oversight. They include the following:

102 Housing Associations

9 Health Authorities

22 local hospital NHS Trusts

26 Governing Bodies of Further Education Colleges

16 Governing Bodies of Grant Maintained Schools

7 Boards of Training and Enterprise Councils (TECs)

1 Urban Development Corporation (in part of Cardiff)

3 Regional Arts Associations

3 National Park Committees

6 Agricultural Training Boards

6 Agriculture Wages Committees

8 Education Business Partnerships

8 Careers Service Companies

What has happened to the Careers Advisory Service is yet one more example of the role and functions of elected local government being eroded. The 1993 Trade Union Reform and Employment Rights Acts removed from local education authorities their statutory duty to provide the careers service. Instead, responsibility has been placed directly with the respective Secretaries of State for Wales, Scotland and England. Initially, there were undertakings that the service would remain with local government. Now it is clear that the intention is to push it into the private sector.

The same trend is observable with the police authorities. The number of elected councillors sitting on them has been reduced and in their place are appointees of the Secretary of State. Moreover, their budgets now come directly from the Welsh Office, instead of being channelled through local government. This is resulting in a widening of the democratic deficit. Local Quangos, for instance, are rarely subject to the accountability mechanisms that apply to local elected councils:

* Councillors are subject to election

* Councillors are liable to surcharge for improper expenditure.

* The local ombudsman can investigate grievances on behalf of individuals.

* Accounts are audited by the Audit Commission.

* Councils must appoint monitoring officers with independent responsibilities for finance and for ensuring probity.

Different standards concerning probity in the management of public money and service delivery apply to elected and non-elected local government, with the more stringent standards generally applying to the elected bodies. Moreover, as has been argued above, a democratic deficit will be opened up in the new system by the joint arrangements that will have to be put in place to ensure the delivery of key services. At most these will be subject to scrutiny by elected members only through indirect mechanisms.

Clause 33 of the Local Government (Wales) 1994 Act contains a general provision under which the Secretary of State has powers until 1999 to direct councils to enter into a joint arrangement for any service which appears in his view to have failed or to be at risk of failure. Clause 34 contains a 'power of last resort' under which a service may be removed from two or more councils and passed to a statutory joint authority which *may* include members of the councils.

It may be argued that these last two clauses are unlikely to be operated and so can be disregarded. If that were the case, why were they included in the legislation? The record of centralisation by central government since 1979, and in particular the general diminution in the powers of local government, suggests that the temptation to use these 'reserve powers' may be strong.

The conclusion can only be that, under the new system, democracy is indeed in the balance in the Wales of the 1990s. This will remain the case unless and until

> * The twenty-two new councils are able to use their enabling and purchasing role in service delivery to claw many functions, such as those in the health service, back into elected control;
>
> * The democratic deficit is addressed at the all-Wales level.

When an Assembly or Parliament for Wales is established the powers, structure and —crucially — the financing of local government should be looked at again. There are far more appropriate structures to suit the needs of Wales than twenty-two unitary authorities that are unitary in name only. A better approach would be democratise the tiers that actually exist. This might entail re-establishing perhaps around fifteen strategic counties. This could be combined with a return to the old urban and rural district councils. These last could replace the present relatively powerless Community Councils and be given a real job of work to do in local planning, housing and education. They could emerge as the key instrument of a truly local, democratic government more closely in touch with the many natural communities of Wales. At the same time effective and autonomous finance for local government should be implemented, based on a progressive local income tax. Therein lies the subject matter for an intense debate that could only properly be carried through by a directly elected Welsh government.

NOTES

1. Gwilym Jones, speech to a Local Government Forum at Cardiff City Hall, organised by the Welsh Association of Community and Town Councils, 12 November 1994. The text is carried in the inaugural issue of *The Welsh Democracy Review*, Summer 1995 (The Parliament for Wales Campaign, 11 Gordon Road, Roath, Cardiff).
2. Welsh Office consultation paper, *The Structure of Local Government in Wales*, June 1991.
3. This paper is attached as an Annex to a report produced by the Secretariat to the Welsh Consultative Council on Local Government [ELC (92) 16] in August 1992. This, and other related documents quoted here, are in the possession of the Welsh local authority associations. The paper quoted at this point continues:

> Purchasing can be done at different levels. At one extreme an authority might decide to provide many services itself and purchase no more than is necessary to comply with requirements laid upon it in specific service areas. At the other, an authority might decide to purchase an entire service or package of services (and possibly the specialist advice and skills to run it or them) — employing directly only the strategic management, planning and purchasing skills necessary to determine and specify service need, then to negotiate a contract or contracts to ensure that need is met and finally to monitor the delivery of the service. Many other purchaser/provider models can be envisaged between these two extremes.
>
> Providers and potential providers might comprise local authorities, separate units set up by authorities individually or in consortia, other public bodies, the voluntary sector, and commercial organisations. Together, these form a pool of available capacity from which purchasers can select in securing services. In some instances, it may be sensible for groups of purchasers to collaborate to secure a service or package of

> services; to be in a position to be able to do this effectively, they may well need to share experiences and develop flexible working alliances of varying complexity. As the enabling function develops, so will the dynamic partnerships between purchasers; and also between purchasers and providers ...
>
> The enabling function is thus a key element of the strategic planning and management of services. It forms the route whereby the body responsible for the delivery of services (i.e. each unitary authority within its area) is able to take well-informed decisions on behalf of client groups, purchase services for them from the most appropriate source, and remain fully accountable for the range and quality of the services which are made available.

4. *Municipal Journal*, 8-14 January, 1993.
5. Personal communication to the author, August 1995.
6. See, for example George A. Boyne et al. *Local Government Reorganisation: A Review of the Process in Scotland and Wales* (Rowntree publications, 1995).
7. *Western Mail*, 22 November 1994.
8. There are powerful arguments — and not least those of democratic accountability — persuading in the direction of this second option. These are laid out fully in recent discussion documents produced by the Council of Welsh Districts, *The Future of Local Government in Health Care Purchasing*, June 1995, and by the Association of Metropolitan Authorities in England entitled *The Future Role of Local Authorities in the Provision of Health Services*, September 1994.

VICEROYS ON THE MAKE

Since the Welsh Office was established in 1964 a perennial question has been the extent to which its leading Minister represents Wales in Whitehall, or Whitehall in Wales. The appointment of a succession of Secretaries of State for Wales representing English constituencies has strengthened the view that since 1979 the balance has tilted sharply in the Whitehall direction. Resentment has also been fuelled by the appointment of personalities distinctly out of sympathy with Welsh aspirations, most notably John Redwood. As a result the position of Secretary of State has widely come to be seen as akin to a colonial-style Governor General or even Viceroy.

John Redwood's appointment, in May 1993, drew a predictable response in these terms. Labour's Shadow Secretary of State, Ron Davies, said:

> This appointment will be resented even by Tories in Wales. It is abundantly clear that John Major has written off the Tory party in Wales, accepting that they have no mandate, by replacing an out-of-touch governor general with a city slicker.[1]

Four months later it was revealed that Redwood had spent only one night in Wales since his appointment — to attend the Welsh Conservative Conference at Llangollen. This revelation prompted Plaid Cymru's President Dafydd Wigley to comment:

> The job is becoming more and more that of a governor general and losing sight of its original purpose of being a voice for Wales in the Cabinet.[2]

That John Redwood was using his Welsh Office position to project his own, often eccentric, agenda, was dramatised when he launched his bid for the Conservative leadership in the summer of 1995. It was felt by some in the party after this failed that a return to the Welsh Office would be a just desert. Instead, he was sacked and replaced with another Englishman, William Hague. Aged thirty-four and representing the Richmond constituency in Yorkshire, Hague's main claim to fame hitherto had been a rousing speech to the 1977 Conservative Conference, when he was 16. He appeared to be given the Welsh post to gain experience for eventual higher office.

A former Labour Secretary of State for Wales, John Morris, remarked, 'Not since Caligula made his horse senator has there been such a ridiculous appointment'.[3] The response of Eleri Carrog, chair of Siarter Cymru (the Welsh branch of the constitutional reform group, Charter 88) was more considered:

> This is the fourth successive appointment of an English MP with no Welsh background to run Wales. The very basis of democracy is the idea of being represented, and there is no way that William Hague represents the Welsh people.[4]

The contradiction inherent in the appointment of such unrepresentative figures has created its own paradox, however. In highlighting differences between the Welsh and English, the British political centre has done much to promote the very sense of separateness it wants to contain. Though the Welsh Office by now is more of an outpost of Whitehall in Wales than the other way round, that in itself has served to promote the country's distinctiveness. As Lord Elis Thomas has written:

> The most striking feature of the Welsh Office for Welsh media watchers is that it has become the most prominent place in Wales in which to protest. Demonstrations about everything from the Government's policy in the Middle East and the Gulf War across to the closure of the smallest one-class primary school ... are acted out in front of that building. This is the actually existing government of Wales. It is the state of Wales. Secretaries of State for Wales, particularly the previous incumbent (Peter Walker) acted as if they were prime ministers of Wales. Flanked by motor cycle outriders speeding out of Stuttgart, on yet another European high tech trail. And what were these outriders there to protect him against?[5]

The value of John Redwood's brief tenure in Wales was that his personality and the gesture politics he promoted, served to highlight for the Welsh people their own sense of themselves as separate from the government they were enduring. Unlike his immediate predecessors, John Redwood, the MP for Wokingham, seemed self-consciously to avoid establishing a warm rapport with Wales. It may have been unfortunate, but perhaps excusable, when the television cameras caught him mumbling and stumbling over the words of the Welsh national anthem at the Llangollen Conservative conference in 1993 — a BBC Wales news clip that was endlessly repeated on Britain-wide television during his leadership bid. There was, however, no excuse for failing to discover the pronunciation of well-known Welsh place-names, especially those with such a political resonance as, say, the Rhondda. In the House of Commons he repeatedly referred to this as though it was spelt with one 'd'. 'New man's only link is the M4', was the *Western Mail*'s headline on his appointment as Secretary of State, and that emphatically remained the case during the whole of his tenure of the post. It was partly a matter of personality. Former Tory MP Matthew Parris described him in his *Times* column as

> ... a new creature, half-human, half Vulcan, brother of the brilliant, cold-blooded Spock ... One is left wishing that, just once he might fart, burp or forget to shave.[6]

FOR WALES SEE BRITAIN

John Redwood left a clear impression of being irritated by the backwardness of many parts of the United Kingdom beyond his Home Counties patch. If only Wales could be more like Wokingham, seemed the sub-text of many of his pronouncements. What could that have meant? The journalist Maureen Freely has said that when she knew him in the early 1980s his favourite description of 'backward Britain' was that it was scruffy, revelling in a down-at-heel dependency culture that was holding the whole country back, rather than aspiring to the clean, bright, competitive and entrepreneurial ideal of the forward-looking, prosperous Britain with which he identified.[7]

And, indeed, in his inaugural address as Secretary of State, to the Llangollen Conservative conference, he urged Wales to be more like Wokingham:

> To those who compare Wokingham and Tredegar as if

> condemning Wokingham for daring to succeed, I say I want Tredegar and the Valleys to understand and share more of Wokingham's success.

In the speech he continually described Wales as a region — unlike John Major at the same conference who referred to Wales as a country, and Sir Wyn Roberts, then Minister of State at the Welsh Office, who said Wales was a nation. 'There is a region of the UK I have come to envy,' Redwood said,

> A region where owner occupation is above the national average, where unemployment is below the average ... A region where almost every home has a television and a refrigerator, where 84 per cent have a phone, 82 per cent central heating, two-thirds have a video and 59 per cent a microwave, the highest figure in the UK. Oh yes, and the region also has room for one quarter of the UK's sheep ....[8]

John Redwood inherited from his predecessors Peter Walker and David Hunt a bold initiative in establishing what some have described as the beginnings of a Welsh foreign policy involving the Welsh Office, the Welsh Development Agency, local authorities and the University of Wales. A Brussels office to represent Wales within the institutions of the European Union was established in the early 1990s. Economic and cultural agreements were negotiated with the leading four 'Motor' Regions — Baden-Wurttemberg, Rhônes Alpes, Lombardy and Catalunya. 'Wales is becoming an important player on the international stage,' declared the long-serving Minister of State at the Welsh Office, Sir Wyn Roberts, as he signed the latest Declaration of Co-operation, with Lombardy in February 1994.

Yet only weeks earlier, in a calculated rebuff to this thrust of policy, John Redwood ordered the Welsh Development Agency to drop the marketing theme 'Wales in Europe' from its promotional literature. Instead, in accordance with his Unionist and Europhobic outlook, he insisted the WDA print brochures emphasising that Wales was an integral part of the UK. The Union flag rather than Y Ddraig Goch was to be given pride of place in the literature. This was on the grounds that foreign investors were supposedly confused by material emphasising that Wales was a dynamic small nation in a borderless European Union.[9]

A contrary view was taken by the Assembly of Welsh Counties in evidence it gave to the Welsh Affairs Select Committee when it was conducting an investigation into 'Wales and Europe'. The Counties said Welsh interests were being damaged by the Welsh Office's 'ambiguous relationship with the European Union' which should 'reflect more the views of Wales and not of the UK as a whole':

> The first general task is to continue to highlight the very existence of Wales as a distinct unit within the UK and different from the other component parts. Appropriate action would be for all representatives from any part of Wales at meetings with the Commission or with other European bodies to underline their Welsh connections in discussion, through use of the flag etc. One of our unique features is the language and it may be helpful to bring this out in appropriate circumstances. The Assembly of Welsh Counties, for example, has insisted that at international conferences and meetings its representatives are described as from 'Cymru/Wales' to underline our bilingual nature and distinctiveness from representatives from the rest of the UK.[10]

THE GLOBAL MARKET PLACE

'The winds of global change blow through Wales' new economic valleys,' was John Redwood's favourite theme as Secretary of State. This breathless vision was outlined in many speeches, for example one he made at the opening of a new Business Park at Llandarcy:

> If the streets of London were once paved with gold, let the streets of Cardiff be ringed with gold as the fibre optic networks of the future take ever more information, television programmes and other services ... The issue for the business of the future will not be where does this office lie geographically on the surface of the world but how well is this office connected to the world market by good quality telecoms links backed up by the right information technology.[11]

The Global Marketplace: Capitalism and its Future was the title of a book John Redwood published during his time as Secretary of

State for Wales.[12] In it he identified 'cultural difference' as being a key problem for communities like Wales in coming to terms with the global economy. Yet it was a barrier that could easily be overcome since, he says

> Cultural difference is just one more product variation in the advance of global style and the global market-place.

If this book had not been written a year before his appointment, he would surely have deleted one example he gave of the dangers of resisting the growth of world capitalism. Based on his experiences holidaying in Gwynedd it led to a good deal of embarrassment:

> Special language betrays special thoughts ... If an Englishman enters a shop in Welsh-speaking parts of Wales the locals are likely to switch promptly to speaking Welsh. Thus the Englishman cannot be sure whether they are talking about him.

The point of this observation, he continues, is 'The art of balancing the world market which people want to belong to with the separate identities which they think matter very much.' If there is doubt where John Redwood would place the emphasis in any conflict between the two, the attitude he displayed towards environmental issues during his stewardship in Wales should dispel it. At one level he made all the right signals, for example publishing an *Environmental Agenda for Wales* in January 1995.

Yet this came against a background of mounting controversy in which Redwood had bracketed environmentalists with 'European neo-Nazis' and 'totalitarians in China' as enemies of democracy and capitalism. He was frustrated with the activities of the Countryside Council for Wales which had opposed him on several major developments, including the Cardiff Bay Project which threatens a Site of Special Scientific Interest.[13] In 1994-5 he cut the Council's budget by £3m, some 16 per cent, entailing a phased reduction in staff from 355 to 240. Rumours floated in the Press that he was even contemplating privatising the Snowdonia National Park. As a result a lobby representing four million people and comprising the National Trust, the Royal Society for the Protection of Birds, the Botanical Society of the British Isles,

Greenpeace, the Council for British Archaeology, and the Youth Hostels Association sent a joint letter to the Prime Minister warning him that Redwood's policies were not only threatening wildlife and their habitats but also threatening to breach the law.[14]

The Countryside Council's director of Research and Policy Development at the time, Gareth Wyn Jones, later issued a stinging rebuke of his own. Much had been done, he said, to create a common vision for the future of the Welsh countryside amongst both the public and voluntary sectors in Wales:

> That this should be threatened by the undemocratic actions of a single individual, with little knowledge of or interest in rural Wales, is a tragedy.[15]

'We're heaving a sigh of relief,' said Merfyn Williams, Director of the Council for the Protection of Rural Wales, when Redwood left the Welsh Office.[16] That might be premature since one of William Hague's first acts as Redwood's successor was to rubber-stamp his decision to allow open-cast slate mining at Rhosydd in the heart of the Snowdonia National Park — a decision condemned by the Council for National Parks as well as conservationists in Gwynedd.[17]

APPEASING THE NATIVES

In Wales environmental and linguistic issues are closely related. John Redwood revealed his hand when, notoriously, he refused to sign letters written on his behalf in Welsh. Interviewed by the magazine Golwg in September 1994, he was asked whether he thought using the Welsh language was a matter of choice or a right. 'I've not thought about those two ideas,' he replied.

Maybe it was this question that prompted him to give the language more consideration. In any event, shortly after this interview John Redwood took the highly unusual step of sending the magazine an unsolicited article offering his thoughts on the roots of Welsh identity, calling in aid the nationalist writers Saunders Lewis, Waldo Williams, Gwenallt and Emyr Humphreys. In the article he provided evidence that he had read the poets, at least in translation. He suggested that there is a Welsh tradition, including the language, which we can all share, quoting Saunders Lewis, approvingly, from his poem 'Buchedd Garmon':

> Wales is a vineyard given me to care for,
> To pass on to my children
> And my children's children
> An eternal inheritance.

The language is part of this 'eternal inheritance', Redwood continued:

> It prospers amongst its speakers and lives on as an intonation and inflection amongst the non-Welsh speakers. It is an element in which to live the life of Wales.

Redwood's central point was the reassuring one that this inheritance had survived many disruptions in the past and would do so again. The coming of the coal industry in the nineteenth century, for instance, had disrupted the peasant culture of rural Wales, which many looked back on as a golden age:

> Many feared that the Arcadian Wales, the rural paradise of so many poems would be shattered, destroyed for ever by coal pits and furnaces of the iron age. A new culture of miners and steelworkers were nurtured in Merthyr and grew up in the Valleys of Glamorgan and Gwent. In its wake came the great wealth of the iron-masters, and periods of a redundant market and poverty. A tradition of industrial protest echoed the feelings of rural protest of an earlier period.

Yet just as the old rural Wales had been lost in the nineteenth century, so the twentieth century had seen the ending of the coal industry and a further 'all-perpetuating feeling of loss, the fear that nothing will come to take the place of jobs which offered good pay ...' Redwood says, however, that we should not fear. Alongside the loss had been a renewed growth in the history, language, culture and rural roots of Wales, reflecting the uncertainty following the closing of one episode in the industrial part of the country:

> The tradition, language, culture and identity of Wales

> are renewed and are adapted constantly — just as the bardic traditions were re-devised so cunningly by Iolo Morgannwg for the revived Eisteddfod of the eighteenth century. Representing the continual strands of Welsh history to the modern world is just as remarkable as their deep roots. Under the thin veneer of culture, the ancient power remains — the enigma of Robert Graves' storyteller who ends 'A Welsh incident' with the line 'I was coming to that'. Cymru has been empowered by its rural past. It has profited from the mining period and has learnt from it. It knows that renewal means, as Waldo said: 'Keeping house / In a cloud of witnesses'. The future is there to grasp: a future where the power of Wales will be increased by the skills and experiences of the people of Wales. Wales has nothing to fear of the future: there is a world to be won and a Wales to love.

What are we to make of this extraordinary outpouring, full of nationalist-sounding sentiment, from a Right-wing English ruler during a temporary sojourn in Wales? It is a question considered by the historian John Davies, who in the same issue of *Golwg* reflected that:

> It has to be borne in mind that Redwood is a fellow of All Souls, the headquarters of appeasement policy — the attempt to avoid confrontation with Hitler by reconciliation. Is this an attempt at reconciliation? Is the message, 'Don't be nasty to me — perhaps Dafydd ap Gwilym is not my bedside reading, but I'm working my way through the translations of Clancy and Conran'?
>
> But there is another message here, too. Mr Redwood is a right-wing radical. He is not a conservative, but a man who wishes to change society. In the last decades, Welsh historians have embraced the idea that Wales has survived all the crises of its history by re-inventing their nation time after time. In fact, I'm guilty of using the same idea myself. If re-invention is on the agenda why can't Wales be re-invented according to the right's radical ideas? 'Don't fear the future,' says Mr Redwood. 'I'm with you'.
>
> I suppose this is the motivation. But the content is a rehashing of arguments presented over a century ago. When giving his lectures on Celtic history in 1865, Matthew Arnold claimed that the essence of the genius of the Celts was magic and that their spirituality was a

> vital part of the 'eclectic imperial graces' (to quote Tecwyn Lloyd) which was the basis of Britain's greatness.
>
> 'Don't worry that the coal industry has gone,' Mr Redwood said. 'You have spiritual values.'

THE WELSH STAGING POST

There is no doubt that Redwood's appointment was determined more by the need to bring some right-wing ballast into the Cabinet than by any Welsh considerations. The Cabinet reshuffle of May 1993 put three Europe-minded interventionists at the heart of the government's economic policy-making — Kenneth Clarke as Chancellor, Michael Heseltine as President of the Board of Trade, and David Hunt as Secretary of State for Employment. Redwood, along with Michael Howard (Home Secretary), Peter Lilley (Social Security) and Michael Portillo (Chief Secretary to the Treasury) were the only unadulterated Thatcherites left in key positions. Among them were to be found John Major's 'bastards', to quote his celebrated off-the-record comment picked up during a television interview in the summer of 1993. Undoubtedly one of them was John Redwood.

At the Tory Party conference in October 1993 it was these Ministers who established Major's 'Back to Basics' agenda. But it was John Redwood who had got their first with a speech attacking the alleged increase and profligacy of single mothers in Cardiff the previous June.[18] A question raised by this sequence of events is: was Redwood responding spontaneously to the situation he found on the ground in the St Mellons Housing Estate, or was he consciously and deliberately setting a new Conservative agenda that would place him at the forefront of attention?

That the latter is the correct interpretation was supported by another speech Redwood made a few months later, to Conservative students at Reading University, in November 1993. He reiterated his attack on single teenage mothers who needed to be told 'of the responsibilities and costs of parenthood, not left to see children as a passport to a separate home and income.' In addition he attacked trendy left-wing teaching methods and 'political correctness', and demanded a crusade against 'fashionable' ideas being peddled by 'establishment intelligentsia' working in the public sector. He also took a swipe at clergy who brought politics into the pulpit. 'When people go to Church at Christmas or Easter they want to hear about Christ's birth and his conquest of death,' he said. 'Far fewer go to hear the vicar give another sermon on benefits policy between the great feasts.'

An advantage of the post of Secretary of State for Wales is that its wide responsibilities allow the holder to speak out on a broader range of issues than other, often higher ranking Ministers. All holders of the office, have made use of it in this way. John Redwood dramatically illustrated the virtues of the position when he used it as a launching pad for his assault, albeit abortive, on the Conservative leadership. Transparently he was a Viceroy on the make. In the process he achieved one thing that might have been thought impossible — the unifying of the Opposition in Parliament. As Cardiff West Labour MP Rhodri Morgan put it:

> He used Wales not as a laboratory for Thatcherite policies, but as a platform for right-wing theorising. He was fairly pragmatic in what he did, but he made these extreme statements to play to a narrow band within the M25.[19]

NOTES

1. *Western Mail*, 28 May 1993.
2. *Western Mail*, 12 October, 1993.
3. *Western Mail*, 6 July 1995.
4. *Western Mail*, 7 July 1995.
5. Dafydd Elis Thomas, Lord Nant Conwy, 'The Constitution of Wales', in Bernard Crick (ed.) *National Identities* (Oxford: Political Quarterly/Blackwell, 1991) p.65.
6. See Andrew Roth, *Parliamentary Profiles*, PPSL, 1994, p. 1225-9.
7. *The Guardian*, 6 January 1994.
8. Conservative Central Office press release, June 1993.
9. 'Redwood stifles Welsh initiative in Europe', *The Independent*, 28 January 1994.
10. Assembly of Welsh Counties, *Evidence to the Welsh Affairs Committee on Wales and Europe*, 23 June 1995.
11. Welsh Office Press Release, 1 September 1994.
12. Harper Collins, January 1994.
13. See Robert Minhinnick (ed.) *Green Agenda - essays on the environment of Wales* (Bridgend: Seren, 1994) p.141-3.
14. See report in *The Independent on Sunday*, 19 February 1995.
15. Gareth Wyn Jones, 'What future for the Countryside Council for

Wales?', *Planet* No. 112, August 1995, p.112-3.
16. Geoffrey Lean, 'Hague assuages green anger over Redwood', *The Independent on Sunday*, 30 July 1995.
17. 'Snowdonia slate mine fury', *Western Mail*, 16 August 1995.
18. In his speech Redwood alleged that 65 per cent of the mothers on the St Mellons Estate were single — a quick soundbite that received full atention from the London media. Cardiff City Council's housing department later reported the true figure — 17.5 per cent, but by then the story had died. Redwood continued the theme, even after he had resigned as Welsh Secretary, attempting to create a 'moral panic' around the issue. Thus in an article in *The Mail on Sunday* (13 August 1995) he said young unmarried mothers should put their children up for adoption if their immediate family was unable to support them. Redwood was immediately attacked for gratuitous seeking of headlines, a fair claim since the scale of the problem was actually reducing at the time. According to the latest statistics, for 1992, the number of teenagers who become pregnant in England and Wales went down to 7, 254, the lowest figure since 1970 (*The Guardian*, 15 August, 1995)
19. Quoted in *The Observer*, 2 July 1995.

GOING NATIVE

It is only, perhaps, a Welsh politician who could be described as having 'gone native' in his own country. Yet this was the view of Ron Davies, MP for Caerphilly and Shadow Secretary of State for Wales, according to un-named Labour sources reported by the *Western Mail* in April 1995. In the report, 'gone native' was defined as Ron Davies seeing himself 'as a sort of Welsh left-wing crusader, setting the agenda for New Labour in Wales, however at odds his vision might be with that of the party leadership in London'.[1]

The view from London was that far from representing 'New' Labour, Ron Davies typified the unreconstructed past. This became clear when he organised a boycott of Welsh questions in the House of Commons in protest at the appointment of William Hague as Secretary of State for Wales. 'This protest is just the type of infantile leftism which Tony Blair has always avoided and which "new" Labour was supposed to have abandoned,' was the view of *The Times*.[2] In fact the action, because it also won the support of Plaid Cymru and the Liberal Democrats, did much to highlighted the issue, albeit in the form of ritual denunciations by the Press: 'It achieved nothing except to deprive Welsh Labour MPs, and hence their constituents, of one of their monthly chances to question Welsh ministers,' *The Times* continued. That was the London viewpoint (echoed faithfully by the *Western Mail*). From a Welsh perspective, however, what was to be gained by questioning a person who could have nothing useful to say about Welsh affairs, other than mouth the platitudes of his civil servants?

The protest did much to confirm the perception that Ron Davies was changing Labour's approach to Wales. Under his leadership the balance between a Welsh and British outlook has moved. Certainly, his rhetoric has signalled a profound shift. It is difficult to imagine any comparable Welsh Labour leader in recent decades addressing the British Labour conference in the terms Ron Davies used at Blackpool in 1994:

> Like the Scots we are a nation. We have our own country. We have our own language, our own history, traditions, ethics, values and pride ... We now in Wales

> demand the right to decide through our own democratic institutions the procedures and the structures and the priorities of our own civic life.

That statement can only be fully understood against the background of Ron Davies' slow maturing as a politician. He has always operated pragmatically, and in response to concrete problems and situations. Yet a study of his record shows a guiding principle has been democracy, one that he brought to a recalcitrant Labour Party in the Rhymney Valley in the 1970s and is now bringing to Wales as a whole in the 1990s. In this he can be seen as a moderniser in the best sense of that term. There is both irony and injustice, therefore, in his being portrayed by some in the Blair camp as typifying the old sclerotic Labour of smokestack Britain and its block vote mentality. For that is something Ron Davies has consistently fought against.

LOCAL ROOTS

Ron Davies has the same Valleys background as his early mentor, Neil Kinnock. Brought up in Machen in the 1950s he went from Bassaleg Grammar School (near Newport) to study Geography and Geology at Portsmouth Polytechnic in the 1960s. Returning to Wales he worked in further education with the old Monmouthshire County Council and then with the Workers Education Association. In the 1970s he deferred to Kinnock's opposition to the devolution proposals of that decade, but thereafter their paths diverged. When Neil Kinnock became an MP at the 1970 general election, aged 29, he in effect left Wales for London. Kinnock's Welshness became something to be deployed as an attitude and accent that drew attention within the Labour movement but was ultimately a handicap outside. Removed from his roots Kinnock lost authenticity.

Ron Davies's experience has been more firmly grounded in experience of local government and he has developed, if gradually and pragmatically, a more deep seated Welsh consciousness. In 1971, at the age if 24 he became the youngest council leader in Britain, running Bedwas and Machen Urban District Council. In the early 1970s he led that Council's rearguard action, along with Clay Cross in Yorkshire, against the Conservative government's efforts to raise council house rents. Bedwas and Machen was a small community of 12,000 people that had a surplus on its housing account. Yet the 1972 Housing Finance Act required the Council to increase its rents by 50p a week followed by another £1 in 1973. The council refused and a commissioner was sent in to impose the increases. During the ensuing campaign of opposition the Bedwas and Machen Labour Party won two by-elections in seats previously held by Independent councillors. 'The experience taught me the importance of taking people with you,' Ron Davies recalled. 'If you go to people and explain what you are doing you can take a radical position and win'.[3]

However, in the local elections of 1976 for the new Rhymney Valley Council, created as a result of the 1974 reorganisation, Labour lost. Plaid Cymru took control with 23 seats, along with six Independents , to Labour's 19. Aged 30 and still the youngest among his fellow Labour councillors Ron Davies went into opposition. The period taught him that a political party must continually renew itself if it is to succeed. 'Ever since I've been active I've been an arch-moderniser,' he said. 'I have been forever trying to get the Labour Party to come to terms with the reality of what was happening to it'.

In the Rhymney Valley in the late 1970s the party split. The constituency's MP, Fred Evans — one of the 'Gang of Six' MPs who were opposing devolution (see Chapter 1) — announced he would not be contesting the forthcoming general election. There was a classic confrontation for the succession, between Ron Davies, seen as on the Left, and the constituency secretary the late Bob Blundell, a Geography Lecturer at the University College of Wales, Cardiff, who represented the traditional Right. Blundell's supporters, seeing that Ron Davies might win, drafted in Ednyfed Hudson Davies, the former Conwy MP (1966-70), who won the nomination by three votes. Not long after the 1979 general election, however, the constituency's boundaries were re-drawn to include Ron Davies' Bedwas and Machen. Hudson Davies saw the writing on the wall and resigned to join the new Social Democratic Party. Ron Davies then won the nomination and became Caerphilly's MP at the 1983 general election.

Meanwhile, Labour had won back control of the Rhymney Valley district council from Plaid Cymru at the 1979 local elections. Ron Davies, leading the council once more, had to confront old Labour tactics. These were to punish voters in wards that had failed to return Labour councillors — by denying spending on projects such as leisure centres and parks — and to refuse to allow opposition councillors membership of council committees. It was a testing ground for democratic politics. Ron Davies argued and won the case for proportional representation for parties on council committees.

THE ROAD TO WELSH AWARENESS

During the 1970s Ron Davies was agnostic on devolution. Immersed in local politics he was sceptical about such a radical change so soon after the reorganisation of local government, and the creation of a two-tier structure, in 1974. There was very little debate in the constituency parties, the government in London were preoccupied with other things, the counties and districts were arguing amongst themselves, European elections were looming, and a formidable group of MPs led by Neil Kinnock were taking a strong line against the party's official policy. 'The time did not seem right, so I kept my head down and voted No,' was how Ron Davies summed up his position in the 1979 referendum.

The balance shifted in the mid-1980s, under the impact of the Thatcher government, and particularly in the wake of the 1987 election. 'Like everybody I was pretty deflated after that result,' Ron Davies recalled:

> I felt the future was bleak. We had delivered in Wales, winning seats like Cardiff West and Clwyd South West. If England had performed as well we would have won the election. There was this very strong feeling that democracy was being undermined. A system of representation is contradicted when a country like Wales can vote one way and be delivered something completely different. Touring my constituency the day after the vote I came across graffiti on a railway bridge in Nelson — 'We voted Labour, we got Thatcher!' That summed the whole thing up for me. This question of democracy — the question of Welsh representation — confronted me as a political reality which we had to address.

It was a key moment, one that as he says, exemplifies his

response to politics. He does not start from an ideological standpoint, but from pragmatic reality and the need to discover ways of dealing with it. Then Westminster politics intervened. Since 1984 he had served in the Labour whips office in the Commons but from the start, and along with a group of junior whips, he had not seen eye to eye with the chief whip Derek Foster. He was continually trying to make its operation more efficient and up-to-date, introducing computers into the office in 1984 for instance. There was a clash of generations. Ron Davies was sacked as a whip by Foster in 1988, but immediately promoted to the Front Bench as a spokesman on Food, Agriculture and Rural affairs by Neil Kinnock.

This position, which he held until the 1992 general election, might seem incongruous for a Welsh Valleys MP. However, that belies the reality that his constituency is largely rural and that he himself lives in an old farmhouse and spend muc time in the surrounding countryside. He is a member of and advocate for the Royal Society for the Protection of Birds. This last organisation has more members in Wales than all the political parties combined. It may have accounted, at least in part, for Ron Davies' initial opposition to the Cardiff Bay Barrage.

During these years he set about establishing a green agenda for Labour, built on agricultural concerns. He was the first to raise the problem of BSE infection as an example of low British standards on food safety when compared with continental Europe. He raised concerns about animal welfare before they became fashionable, and also marked out the interface between the environment and farming that was to become a central concern of rural politics in the 1990s. He popularised, if not invented, the notion of a 'Green premium'.

Somewhere along the line of this trajectory through the 1980s and into the early 1990s Ron Davies's whole approach to Wales was transformed. A preoccupation with the environment and the landscape of Wales had something to do with it. The birth of his daughter, Angharad in 1986, was another dimension. She began attending Ysgol Feithrin — a Welsh-medium playgroup — and later a Welsh-medium primary school. By the early 1990s Ron Davies was learning Welsh himself and studying at the Nant Gwytheyrn residential Welsh learners' centre in Gwynedd. He says he was always aware of the Welsh language in his family history. Both his mother's parents were Welsh-speaking and his paternal grandfather, from a farming background in the lower Rhymney Valley, was also Welsh speking.

> I was conscious, too, of the Welsh names of the farms and lanes in the area. I always regretted that I had no Welsh. But when I went to school in Monmouthshire, in the 1950s, teaching Welsh was not even contemplated, not even in the Machen primary school. Welshness meant half-a-day's holiday on St David's Day.

SHADOW SECRETARY OF STATE

Ron Davies was elected to the Shadow Cabinet in 1992 and Secretary of State for Wales by the late John Smith. At that point the Welsh Labour party had made no significant intervention into the world of policy-making or political ideas for more than a decade. After the 1979 referendum, which had split the Welsh Labour movement asunder, the party seemed afraid of movement in any direction for fear of fresh strife breaking out. The trade unions, which had been led so radically by the newly-created Wales TUC in the 1970s, was driven into a series of defensive actions over a succession of steel and coal closures. The leadership of the Welsh party was distinguished for its lack-lustre failure to engage with contemporary events, let alone any attempt at mobilising a new vision.

Momentarily, during the 1984-5 miners' strike, the Wales Congress in Support of Mining Communities, seemed to offer hope of a new beginning. At its opening rally, in Cardiff's City Hall in October 1984, the late South Wales Miners' leader, Emlyn Williams, said that when he had been first told about the movement he thought it was intended as some kind of surrogate Welsh Assembly. Though he appreciated that its objectives were less far-reaching than that, it still carried lessons for the future: 'Had we had devolution — a Welsh Assembly, a Parliament for the people of Wales —we would have had a voice,' he said.[4]

Following the 1987 election, the Wales Labour Party began once more to take this message on board, if extremely tentatively. During the next few years the Welsh Executive held consultations with its constituency organisations and the trade unions on the way forward for a Welsh Assembly, or what it preferred at that stage to describe as a 'regional government' for Wales. The result was proposals, contained in the 1992 manifesto, for an Assembly to be established at the same time as local government was reorganised, replacing the existing 8 counties and 37 districts with a single-tier of between 17 and 25 most-purpose authorities.

This was the policy, but there was little debate or enthusiasm around it. The party's leader was Neil Kinnock who still carried the legacy of the 1970s and who, in any event, had other preoccupations. It was clear that though an Assembly might be a policy, it was not a priority. Crucially, too, advocates for the change had yet to make the radical connection between Welsh democracy and regenerating the Welsh economy. This was becoming clear in Scotland as a cross-party campaign gathered momentum under the umbrella of the Scottish Convention. A key exponent was the late John Smith who was influential in the drafting of Labour's 1989 policy review *Meet the Challenge — Make the Change*. This stated:

> We see the need the encourage each of our nations and regions to build the capacity to sustain their indigenous economy. In some cases, we already have the foundation to build on in the form of regional development agencies. We shall extend their role and supplement it with the creation of a network of regional investment banks. They will be substantially funded by the British Investment Bank, but will also be free to raise further funds through regional bonds. In Scotland the Scottish Assembly will have greatly strengthened powers of intervention through both existing and new government structures, as well as the responsibility for the administration of regional policy and revenue raising powers through the variation of income tax levels...

Such thinking had yet to penetrate Welsh Labour circles. The case for a Welsh Assembly was confined to the need to take over control of the Quangos and give some all-Wales strategic direction to local government. This was the position that faced Ron Davies when he became Shadow Secretary of State in the summer of 1992.

Even so his appointment came at a good moment for launching a fresh initiative. The 1992 election had illustrated yet again the yawning democratic deficit in Wales. Equally important, the

European dimension of Welsh affairs was changing the terms of the argument. 'After the 1992 election any doubts I might have entertained about devolution were completely dispelled,' Ron Davies said:

> I was conscious that there was a growing recognition that the Welsh identity was a resource we had to fall back on in an increasingly complex world in which we were dealing, not just with the European Single Market, but the global economy as well. So I determined to put devolution at the centre of our policy. We had to grasp the issue positively and make it a priority. We had to be for it or against it and if we were in favour we could not be half-hearted. The task was to make the party aware that so many of our other vital concerns — with the economy, education, the health service, the environment, agriculture — all depended on our first achieving the mechanism of a democratic assembly to put our policies into effect.

After the 1992 general election defeat there had been calls for a Welsh Constitutional Convention along Scottish lines, not least from the Wales TUC annual conference. This pressure alarmed the Welsh Executive, mainly because of its nervous attitude towards cross-party collaboration on any issue, and least of all Welsh devolution. Instead, it established its own Policy Commission. This was to take nearly three years to mull over the possibilities before issuing its document *Shaping the Vision*, with its proposals for an Assembly with limited powers, in May 1995.

ECONOMIC DEVELOPMENT AND DEMOCRACY

While this process was underway Ron Davies resolved to provide some leadership. An opportunity came in a speech he gave to a conference on regenerating the Valleys, in Treorchi in the Rhondda in November 1992. He began with an analysis of the failure of traditional regional economic policies to make any impact on the Welsh economy during the 1980s. Regional preferential assistance had been cut by 60 per cent and unemployment had risen by 88 per cent. The most gifted of the young were leaving the Valleys, at a rate of 1,500 a year:

> A community cannot survive if its most gifted leave at the first available opportunity. Without a serious, combined regeneration effort our future will seep away. Apart from emigration, perhaps the biggest single signal of community decline is a soaring crime rate ... Tellingly, one of the most common crimes is car theft — the pastime of the bored teenager with no local entertainment, no transport links after dark, high unemployment, poverty, urban dereliction, weaker family structures and no perceived prospects to succeed ...

A new approach was needed, one that relied on partnership between the public and private sectors, focused on harnessing development from within, and looking to continental Europe for inspiration:

> To regenerate the Valleys we need partnerships, between central and local government, employers and trade unions, and the public and private sectors ... Our new partnerships should draw on the experience of other European regions such as Baden-Wurttemberg in Germany, Rhône-Alpes in France and Lombardy in Italy which have all tackled the switch from heavy industry with a programme that encourages private sector investment with publicly funded infrastructure ... [they] have also recognised the importance of education and high quality training and skills and there is publicly sponsored research and development with new links forged with local universities and colleges that encourage technology transfer, innovation and modernisation ...
>
> Creating a strong infrastructure demands extensive government intervention and European experience teaches us that public sector/private sector partnership can lead to success. I do not believe, however, that all this can be done by us taking a begging bowl to Westminster. It is something that we can and must do for ourselves, so we must have appropriate structures for local accountability and power. The present régime is thoroughly undemocratic and in the middle of it stands the Welsh Office. For a modern economy we need a modern democracy and this should be based on an elected Welsh Parliament and strengthened local councils. A more democratic and responsive Wales is not only right for democracy, it is also needed for the sake of industry, jobs and regeneration.[5]

This was the most radical speech made about Wales by a Labour politician for a generation. By saying Welsh democratic structures and economic regeneration were intimately connected he simultaneously signalled a break with Labour's past attitudes and defined in the sharpest terms Labour's cleavage with the Tories.

The reference to the need for strengthened local councils, alongside the significantly described *Parliament* — another effort to move the debate forward — was further elaborated in a speech he made in Cardiff on the new local government system, in January 1995. By now, however, Ron Davies had been obliged to tone down his terminology in response to the gathering debate inside the party. Henceforth he referred to the all-Wales democratic body under discussion as an *Assembly* (see Chapter 1). Labour, he said, was committed to introducing 'a new power of general competence to local councils'. There was a need to re-assess the balance of powers between central and local government, especially in the light of the concentration of additional powers in the Welsh Office and the dilution of direct democratic control by the proliferation of joint boards:

> I hope, however, that any loss of strategic planning services to the Assembly will be more than compensated for by new and enhanced functions that local authorities will acquire under our proposals. A range of services from education through training to health are good examples of where new democratic systems of public accountability are required ...
>
> We must break down and devolve the centralist state that the UK has now become and the central part of that is that local authorities must be set free from unnecessary and artificial constraints imposed by central government. Local government must be constitutionally independent of the executive and within that context local government now needs to state its vision and to reclaim the powers approved by the executive.
>
> The proper objective of all political parties now should be to ensure that duly elected local authorities are guaranteed their independence beyond the reach of even a Labour government. I do not accept that the man in Whitehall knows best, even if it is a Labour man. Power must be dispersed in a healthy modern and proper democracy and we have to ensure that local

> government is free to carry out its local mandate safe from interference and protected from financial manipulation by central government.[6]

Precisely how this approach might be carried through in the field of housing had been outlined by Ron Davies some months earlier, in a speech to the Welsh Federation of Housing Associations. Acknowledging a severe shortage of new housing, leading to a mounting homelessness problem in Wales, he said the answer was to place local authorities once more at the centre of provision:

> Wales desperately needs local government to be empowered to build and provide low cost housing ... Labour is committed to legislating for a democratic Welsh Assembly in the first year of government. This would give housing policy a democratic and strategic all-Wales voice. Instead of having a Quango [Tai Cymru] responsible for housing within Wales we will put housing back into democratic control ...
>
> We will expect Tai Cymru to work towards establishing Cartref, the housing arm of the Welsh Assembly, and to bring forward plans for the amalgamation of its own organisation with that of the Welsh Office Housing Division. One of the first tasks of the Assembly and Cartref, once it is up and running, will be to develop an all-Wales housing policy. The new Unitary authorities will have the lead role in this process, being responsible as they will be for so much of Welsh housing.
>
> Under Labour the new authorities will become the main agency for provision of a total housing service to the various communities that they serve. These plans will be built across all types of housing tenure and will be the vehicle for developing both public and private sector housing in partnership with various housing bodies including the housing associations.[7]

In these and other speeches Ron Davies laid out a practical vision of how self-governing democratic institutions could be mobilised to improve and modernise the Welsh economy and the range of social provision for the people of Wales. More than this he was conscious that to succeed, such a democratic revolution would require consent and support from the people as a whole, and not just from the Labour movement, important and influential as it is. It was this dimension of his approach that drew the most criticism from people in the party who believed it need not, indeed should not, solicit outside, cross-party alliances and support.

In immediate policy terms this dispute revolved around the argument whether the Assembly should be elected by first-past-the-post or by some other system of proportional representation. Inside the Policy Commission and the Welsh Executive Ron Davies lost this argument in early 1995. However, he made it clear that he would not let it go, adding that the broader the political base of the Assembly the greater its legitimacy would be. The benefit would be a political entrenchment of its powers, making it harder for any future hostile — that is to say, Tory — government at Westminster to weaken, or even abolish them:

> Once the Assembly is established it must reflect the diversity and plurality of Welsh social, political and cultural life. By doing that we will have greater status for the Assembly as a national institution. We can give a clearer focus for the development of our Welsh sense of identity, and it will provide the strongest bulwark against those who would seek to undermine or attack the Assembly for party political reasons.[8]

To those who said Labour's Assembly proposals were too weak — that Wales should immediately have a Parliament with primary legislative and taxation powers — Ron Davies countered that devolution was not a single event, but a 'process'.[9] This had begun in the modern period, with the creation of the Welsh Office in 1964, and would continue with the creation of an Assembly in the late 1990s, to bring the Welsh Office under democratic control. And there was no reason, he said, why the 'process' should not continue after that.

Such, assertive and self-confident declarations account for the accusation that Ron Davies has 'gone native' in his own country. his ideas are too radical for some to stomach. What this means in Welsh Labour terms is that they place more emphasis on the Welshness rather than the Britishness of Wales. They also contradict traditional Welsh Labourism and its politics of demobilisation, for they imply action. Under Ron Davies' leadership a renewed and radical agenda for Wales is being put in place.

There is, of course, resistance — not least from parts of Ron Davies' own southern valleys where notions of pluralism and a Welsh European rather than a British agenda have a subversive ring. There is little doubt, however, that the vitality, even the survival, of Welsh Labour politics depends on the success of this project. Whatever the eventual outcome, Ron Davies was responsible during the mid-1990s for the most creative period in Welsh Labour policy making since the mid-1970s.

NOTES

1. Patrick Fletcher, 'Ron's Vanishing Victory', *Western Mail*, 14 April 1995.
2. Peter Riddell, 'Why Blair needs to sideline Labour's Shadow Cabinet duds', *The Times*, 12 July 1995.
3. Interview with the author, August 1995, as are the following quotations.
4. See John Osmond, 'The Future of the Wales Congress' in *Planet* No. 51, June/July 1985, p.119.
5. Ron Davies, *Regenerating the Valleys: The Partnership Approach*, speech at Treorchi, Rhondda, 20 November 1992.
6. Ron Davies, 'Strengthening Local Democracy in Wales', in Sue Essex and Robin Hambleton (eds.) *Towards Unitary Local Government in Wales*, Department of City and Regional Planning, University of Wales, Cardiff, June 1995.
7. Ron Davies, *Labour's Proposals for Housing in Wales*, Welsh Federation of Housing Associations' Annual Symposium, Llandudno, 29-30 September, 1994.
8.Ron Davies, 'Shaping the Vision', in *The Red Kite*, No 38, June 1995.
9. Wales Labour Party Press Release, 12 May 1995, 1 Cathedral Road, Cardiff.

PARTNERSHIP AND ECONOMIC RENEWAL

A key feature, not to say contradiction of Welsh politics in the 1990s is that while an essentially non-interventionist, free-market and on the whole Euro-sceptic government has been in power at Westminster, the Welsh economy has been allowed to drift in opposing directions. Moreover, this has not been a reflection of who has been in charge at the Welsh Office. It is true that from 1987 to 1993 Peter Walker, followed by David Hunt, encouraged a generally pro-active and pro-European approach. But even with John Redwood the underlying policy thrust remained the same. Redwood altered the tone but not the essence.

The driving force has been the Welsh Office itself, together with the Welsh Development Agency which since the mid-1980s have been responding to a rapidly changing economic environment. United Kingdom regional aid, which had buttressed the Welsh economy since the 1930s, was savagely pruned — cut back by some 70 per cent in the decade to 1992. The character of inward investment, though still crucial to upgrading Wales's manufacturing base, was changing and becoming more difficult to obtain.

For these reasons the Welsh Development Agency revised its 1970s strategy, which had consisted of three pillars: land reclamation, advance factory building and inward investment. In contrast to this emphasis on 'hard' infrastructure, the Agency set a higher premium on the 'soft' infrastructure of business support services such as technology transfer, and skills development. Equally, if not more importantly, it began to pay more attention to the needs of already existing firms, both locally and foreign-owned.

By the late 1980s, too, it had become clear that Wales needed to develop a pro-active European policy. This was necessary to maximise funding opportunities, take advantage of the Single European Market, and encourage collaboration between Welsh and continental European firms, especially those found in the key partner Regions of Baden-Wurttemberg, Lombardy, Rhône Alpes, and Catalunya.

SOCIAL CAPITAL

This thinking coincided with a growing appreciation that 'social capital' is an important ingredient of economic renewal. The networks and patterns of behaviour that facilitate co-operation and trust are an essential resource for any modernising economy. Many regard it as at least as important as the presence of raw materials, a skilled labour force or the attraction of inward investment. One recent authoritative study, for example, judges that 'the success or failure of local development depends largely on a range of invisible factors' that together comprise social capital.[1]

Notions of the *Intelligent Region* reflect a reality for many developing economies that knowledge is their most important strategic resource, and learning its most important process. Research pioneered in Wales has identified key characteristics of the administration of such Regions operating with the framework of the European Union.[2] The creation of the Single European Market and the reform of the European Union's Structural Funds were part of a growing internationalisation of regional economies. In response Regions should:

> (1) Become more pro-active towards the European Union.
>
> (2) Develop closer links between their business and institutional communities.
>
> (3) Elaborate policies to enhance regional innovation potential.
>
> (4) Establish mechanisms for self-monitoring and continuous policy improvement.
>
> (5) Engage increasingly in information-sharing partnerships .[3]

Alongside these requirements is another important resource, as abstract as knowledge and learning, namely trust. At its simplest level trust is extremely valuable because it saves a lot of time and trouble to be able to place reliance on other people's work. Yet one cannot buy trust. It has to be earned through repeated formal and informal transactions. This is especially the case when networks for technological innovation are being developed, as the American political scientist Robert Putnam has emphasised:

> By analogy with notions of physical capital and human capital — tools and training that enhance individual productivity — social capital refers to features of social organisation, such as networks, norms and trust, that facilitate co-ordination and co-operation for mutual benefit. Social capital enhances the benefits of investment in physical and human capital and is coming to be seen as a vital ingredient in economic development around the world.[4]

Economic partnerships provide the milieu within which social capital develops. In Wales we have a wide range of institutions all of which have declared an interest in a partnership approach to the economy. They include the Welsh Office and its key Quangos, especially the Welsh Development Agency; the twenty-two new local authorities; the seven Training and Enterprise Councils; the Wales CBI and Wales TUC, the Further and Higher Education Colleges; more than thirty local enterprise agencies, and more than one hundred community enterprises. The networking that is underway between all these agencies comprises Wales's 'social capital'.

AN ENTREPRENEURIAL COMMUNITY

There is an internally held feeling within Wales, reinforced by stereotypes from outside, that the Welsh are not an instinct-ively entrepreneurial people. Outside impressions are the most emphatic. Thus, for example, *The Financial Times* once stated it as axiomatic that,

> ... the Welsh are not a race of self-starters in business. A drive towards entrepreneurialism is lacking throughout the country so that the lead invariably has to be given by one or other official body.[5]

More recently a report for the Institute of Welsh Affairs baldly stated that,

> An enterprise culture does not exist in Wales at present.

> ... It is a change in the culture which must come first to create a climate in which businesses will thrive and grow.[6]

The authors of the report, all drawn from the business community, were looking ahead to the year 2010 and trying to imagine what would be necessary if Wales was to catch up with the most economically advanced Regions in the European Union. What kind of enterprise culture did they have in mind? Undoubtedly it was an Anglo-American pattern of capitalism motivated by aggressive, risking-taking, dynamic and opportunist individuals — captains of industry and so on.

Yet this relies on an extremely narrow vision of entrepreneurialism. It is unlikely to find much resonance in Wales. In facing their future, societies, like individuals, need to recognise and build on their strengths. One of prime importance for Wales can be described as a culture of solidarity, built around our economic history rooted as it is in farming, mining and heavy industry. This stresses co-operation rather than competition. In that sense it has been thought a sufficient explanation why Wales has on the whole failed to produce entrepreneurs in the Anglo-American mould.[7]

Yet in some fields Wales has produced a seemingly endless roll call of enterprising figures — teachers, preachers, artists and sports personalities of all kinds, and also politicians. Who would deny that such diverse contemporary figures as Barry John, John Toshack, Bryn Terfel, Sian Phillips, Tom Jones, Sir Anthony Hopkins, Janet Price, John Humphreys, Neil Kinnock, Alex Carlile, Dafydd Wigley or Dafydd Iwan are not enterprising? Who would not say the same about leading figures from the recent past such as Arthur Horner, Lloyd George, Aneurin Bevan, Saunders Lewis, Raymond Williams, Richard Burton, Carwyn James, Hugh Cudlipp or Sir Geraint Evans?

The Anglo-American model of thrusting business enterprise is not the only one for a society such as Wales to emulate. There is a more appropriate and successful model to hand, one that stresses a collectivist approach, better suited to Welsh traditions and contemporary circumstances. It is, in fact, to be found in many of the world's most successful economies, and most notably for our purposes in continental Europe.

In Germany, for example, a more communal and partnership

approach towards enterprise prevails than the essentially individualist ethos of the Anglo-American tradition. The French economist, M. Albert, has designated this the 'Rhine model' of enterprise culture, one that places emphasis on collectivism and a strong sense of social and familial obligation, thrift and long-termism — elements typically less well developed in Anglo-American business culture. The Rhine model — it might also be described as the Japanese model — typically embraces the following features:

* Interests of communities precede individual interests.

* Investment in industry is valued more highly than investment in finance.

* Education and training are seen as priorities not luxuries.

* Research into civil rather than military projects is prioritised.

* Income disparities are less pronounced than in most countries.

* An inclination towards high personal and household savings.[8]

It is no coincidence that the most successful of the inward investing firms into Wales tend to be German and Japanese that project an entrepreneurial culture in these terms. The first German factories were opened in Wales in 1966; now there are 55. There were only four Japanese employers in the whole of Britain in 1972, two of them in Wales; now Wales has the largest single agglomeration (more than 40) of Japanese-owned plants in Britain, if not in Europe.[9] One reason that these firms have been attracted to Wales is the co-operation they found between the public and private sectors and trade unions and management, co-operation they have done much to sustain.

A partnership approach goes with the grain of the Welsh industrial tradition, stemming from coal-mining and slate quarrying which characteristically relied on state intervention, co-operation, pooled resources and solidarity. In contemporary Wales these are all qualities that are being re-defined and re-asserted to suit modern conditions. In the process Wales is emulating the continental rather than Anglo-American model of entrepreneurialism.

Evidence that such a model can prove highly successful is found in the heartland German regions, and not least in the most successful of all, Baden-Wurttemberg. Although a few large firms, like Mercedes Benz and Robert Bosch, are important for this strong engineering economy, they in turn benefit enormously from large numbers of small and medium-sized enterprises. In fact more than 90 per cent of Baden-Wurttemberg's manufacturing firms employ less than fifty workers. This Region, whose ten million people have developed a GDP greater than most nation-states, has also developed a robust industrial innovation system. Kevin Morgan, of the University of Wales, Cardiff, who has studied European innovation networks, has listed the main features of Baden Wurttemberg's system as follows :

> * A well-developed research and technology transfer system. This hosts over one hundred decentralised technical support centres, each of which affords small and medium sized firms access to advanced technologies, expert advice and problem-solving facilities.
>
> * A highly effective system of vocational education and training. This ensures that sufficient skills are available so that employers do not have to rely on labour poaching.
>
> * A strong networking culture within the corporate sector. Its main feature is strong buyer-supplier linkages between large and small firms in the Region.
>
> * A deep commitment to public-private sector collaboration. This makes for a more collective and consensual approach to the problems of regional development.
>
> * A high degree of political self-governance, which allows certain policies — in education, culture, training and technology, for example — to be tailored to the needs of the Region. This is an attribute that is becoming ever more important in an era of rapid economic change.[10]

In contrast to the Anglo-American model of industrial enterprise, in which innovation is left almost entirely to market forces, the German approach recognises innovation for what it is, namely a collective social endeavour. Although firms are expected to shoulder the main burden there is a dense network of supporting institutions to assist in the process, which enables even the smaller firms to stay abreast of the latest technologies. This is the model that Wales should seek to follow in the 1990s, adjusting and amending it to suit our own particular circumstances.

INNOVATING IN EUROPE

The European Union is now the milieu within which social capital and an entrepreneurial community has to be created and improved. This can be illustrated by a brief examination of three initiatives undertaken by the Welsh Development Agency and the Welsh Office in the 1990s: the opening of the Wales European Centre in Brussels in 1992; participation in the Eurolink programme, and participation in the European Commission's Regional Technology Plan project.

The Wales European Centre was launched in the teeth of Whitehall opposition as a partnership between the Welsh Development Agency, Training and Enterprise Councils, local authorities and the University of Wales. During the 1980s it had become clear that direct representation in Brussels was necessary to ensure access to information and to project the Welsh interest within the European Commission. It is interesting that the demand was first promoted by the lowest level of Welsh governance, the Community Councils. Their Association convened a national conference on the issue at Swansea in 1985. It took another six years of lobbying and Whitehall infighting before the Wales European Centre was finally established.[11] Within a very short time, however, it proved its worth, as the following examples indicate:

> * It has helped secure a RELAY centre for Wales. Based in the Welsh Development Agency's Cardiff headquarters, with a branch office in north Wales, this is one of only four such centres in the UK. It is designed to boost the relatively low share which Wales receives from European research programmes.
>
> * It assisted in the establishment of the first Electronic

> Data Interchange (EDI) Awareness Centre in the UK in Wales as another joint initiative between the WDA and EU. Electronic Data Interchange, a paperless trading system, is revolutionising the ways in which firms transact with one another. Raising the awareness of this technology, and supporting its diffusion, is an important part of a regional innovation strategy for Wales.

The second initiative — the Eurolink programme — was triggered by the co-operation agreement which Wales signed with Baden-Wurttemberg in March 1990, followed by similar agreements with Lombardy, Rhône-Alpes and Catalunya. Eurolink is designed to provide practical support for technical or commercial joint-ventures between Welsh and continental European firms to exploit the Single Market. Regional co-operation agreements provide the framework for such joint-ventures. By the mid-1990s more than 150 deals had been brokered, many of them involving technology transfer arrangements.

Thirdly, Wales was chosen for inclusion in the Regional Technology Plan project, launched by the European Commission in June 1994. Eight pilot Regions, regarded as relatively underdeveloped or less favoured within the European Union, were selected — Limburg (in the Netherlands), Lorraine (France), Saxony (Germany), Norte (Portugal), Central Macedonia (Greece), Abruzzo (Italy), Castilla y Leon (Spain), and Wales (UK). The project's main objectives are:

* To encourage the chosen Regions to develop a regional innovation process, in which a commonly agreed, bottom-up strategy attuned to specific need is defined.

* To provide a framework and strategy for future technology-related investment.

The Regional Technology Plan is designed to stimulate a collective learning process in the Regions involved. It is an aimed at promoting a partnership approach between private firms, public agencies and a wide array of intermediary institutions in the fields of technology transfer and training provision. It is also a declaration that the initial impetus for regional renewal must come from within the Region. In practical terms this turns on a

Region's networking capacity — that is, the disposition of its institutions to collaborate to achieve mutually beneficial ends.

Wales was invited to participate in the Regional Technology Plan because, in the eyes of the European Commission, it had demonstrated a resolve to upgrade its economy through a collaborative effort between the public and private sectors.[12] That is to say, there was already a well established determination to achieve economic progress by developing partnerships. As the European Commission has stated, the Regional Technology Plan exercise will be most fruitful 'in areas where well-founded co-operation between the private and public sectors is — or can be — established.[13] Early work on the Regional Technology Plan emphasised many gaps in Wales's emerging innovation, networking and partnership structures. In particular, there is an urgent need for a regional structure within Wales for carrying these activities forward, a structure that is already implicit in the organisation of the main agencies involved, but not yet fully carried through.

The Welsh Development Agency team preparing The Regional Technology Plan identified key strengths and weaknesses in the Welsh economy and pointed towards a number of priorities for the future. For example, they found Wales to be relatively well endowed with technology support structures in comparison with many other regions in the UK. Some of the key elements are the 12 Higher Education Institutions, 22 Centres of Expertise, 18 industry/technology clubs, 6 sub-regional innovation centres and 5 science and technology parks. Wales can also count an estimated 100-200 firms believed to be carrying our research and development. While this is a small network it does mean that an embryonic 'innovation system' does exist. On the other hand there were clear problems as well — for instance, the larger firms contribute relatively little towards innovation in Wales. In fact Wales is at the bottom of the mainland UK league table for industry-led research and development investment.[14]

Such shortcomings are being addressed by promoting partnerships between the public and private sectors. As important as the production of the Regional Technology Plan is the process of building a collective learning capacity from the bottom up. The Welsh Development Agency has itself explicitly recognised its role as an innovator and animateur in co-operation with other agencies. In its corporate plan for the later 1990s, for example, it says it:

> ... will encourage the formation of effective local development partnerships between the private sector, local authorities and communities, and support the establishment of long term integrated area development strategies for large scale economic sub regions, thereby securing better co-ordination of public sector resources as well as continuity at a time of change.[15]

The Welsh Development Agency and other public and private agencies are engaged in an important learning experience, absorbing lessons from other European Regions and also from German and Japanese firms that have established themselves in Wales. Much importance is also being attached to inter-regional learning procedures. All of the Regional Technology Plan pilot Regions are expected to share the results of their exercises which will then be disseminated throughout the European Union. In this there will be an important role for EURADA, the European Association of Development Agencies, a federation of some eighty Agencies which has been set up specifically to exchange best practice thinking on regional economic development.

Yet, as Kevin Morgan has argued, more lessons are needed, especially to achieve greater freedom to take further intiatives:

> While the Agency is beginning to learn how to operate as a regional animateur instead of being a glorified property developer, learning to work through a wider network of delivery agencies, it needs to secure more autonomy from its political masters in the Welsh Office. Having failed to regulate the WDA properly in the 1980s, when serious management problems took root, the Welsh Office now seems intent on over-regulating the Agency for past failures.[16]

DEVELOPMENT FROM WITHIN

During the 1980s and 1990s the Welsh economy has been undergoing a massive re-structuring. From a previous reliance on smokestack industries the economy now has a much more balanced profile. More people in Wales now work in electronics than (25,000) in coal and steel combined (20,000). Between 1983 and 1992 Wales attracted more than 300 projects in the Welsh Development Agency's key target areas for diversification —

financial services (now employing 70,000 people), vehicles and components, food processing, telecommunications, aerospace and information technology, and healthcare. More than 400 foreign-owned manufacturing companies now employ almost 30 per cent of the workforce, some 70,000 people. Wales is one of the few countries in the Western world where the proportion of manufacturing jobs is rising.

All this not been achieved without cost, however. There has been a large overall loss of jobs. Since the recession of the early 1980s, when 753,000 Welsh men and women were in full-time jobs (1981) this figure had dropped by 69,000 to 684,000 by the mid-1990s. Modernisation of the manufacturing base has therefore been achieved by a large-scale shedding of labour. And new industries have been attracted to a great extent because of relatively low Welsh wage rates, certainly low in relation to continental Europe but also to the rest of Britain as well. The result has been a growing gap between the better and less less well-off, with the latter concentrated in disadvantaged locations, especially the Valleys. According to an analysis by Ron Davies, the Shadow Secretary of State for Wales, the Welsh economy 1n the mid-1990s was characterised by the following long-term structural weaknesses:

> * Gross Domestic Product per head was 14% below the UK average and is the lowest in mainland Britain. With around 4.8 % of the UK's working population, Wales generated only about 4.3% of the UK's GDP.
>
> * Income per head was 15% below the UK average, again the lowest in mainland Britain. From being top of the economic region pay league in 1979 Wales in the mid-1990s was at the botom.
>
> * Earnings for both sexes were below the UK average and, for men, were the lowest in mainland Britain. Forty per cent of Welsh workers earned below the Council of Europe's Decency threshold which itself was only 68 per cent of average gross weekly wages.
>
> *Unemployment rates in the Valleys and remoter rural areas remained stubbornly high, more than 25 per cent for men in many localities.[17]

Wales has an ageing population, low activity rates, and an

industrial structure which, despite recent improvements, remains skewed to sectors with low productivity and earnings. Relatively low labour costs can no longer be sustained to the same extent in a world economy where countries along the Pacific Rim and in Eastern Europe have much lower wage rates. In addition, many global US and Japanese firms have by now established their main bases within the European Union. Their future investment is likely to be concentrated among smaller companies, many of them component and service suppliers to larger firms. As a result of unification Germany is looking more Eastern Europe than to the western seaboard. For all these reasons Wales can expect a decline of inward investment in future.

But rather than a threat this should be regarded as an opportunity. The results of inward investment, whilst undoubtedly raising technology and skills levels within the Welsh economy, have also tended to bring branch factories rather than head offices and research and development facilities. In the 1980s and 1990s, just as in the 1960s and 1970s, many of Wales's young people have been forced to emigrate to find opportunity and promotion, draining the country of its future leaders. Inward investment is better than no investment at all, and strategic inward investment will undoubtedly have a continuing place in the coming decades. But for Wales to create a balanced economy in the next century, one that builds on our most precious asset — the skills and inventiveness of our people — indigenous enterprise and sustainable development from within must be the guiding strategy.

Indigenous development requires careful planning that recognises the distinctive character of the many communities that make up Wales as a whole. This idea that Wales is a community of communities can be a powerful source of strength in the coming decades. The changing patterns of governance in Wales, in particular the reorganisation of local government into unitary authorities together with the promise of a democratic body — an Assembly or Parliament — provide an opportunity to mobilise the political will to promote economic renewal from within.

A twin-track approach is needed: democratic mobilisation and 'top-down' stimulation at the all-Wales level, combined with 'bottom up' initiatives from local government and the communities it embraces. Utilising this approach an indigenous development-from-within strategy would aim to:

* Raise the levels of education, skills and training.

* Concentrate on innovation in the economy.

* Produce clusters of compatible firms and enterprises.

* Network between enterprises in discrete regional locations and at the all-Wales level.

* Underpin the economy with a strong co-operative community enterprise sector.

Taken together these five components comprise investment in Wales' social capital, the networks and patterns of behaviour and trust that facilitate co-operation and sustainable economic development.

COMMUNITY ENTERPRISE

In many ways the final component of this five-pronged strategy is the most important since it provides an opportunity to bring the most disadvantaged and marginalised people into the mainstream economy. At the same time as the all-Wales level of institutions have been elaborated during the past twenty years a parallel growth in the 'local state' has been underway. This is providing the institutional infrastructure necessary to stimulate a co-operative enterprise culture from below. The agencies that have proliferated include the Training and Enterprise Councils, and a wide variety of enterprise networks and joint ventures, regeneration partnerships, 'technopoles', image and tourism promoters, marketing groups, business development forums and consortiums, media and film projects, access projects for youth and the disadvantaged, manufacturing groups, and information technology financial services initiatives. Alongside, and often working in close collaboration with these, are around a hundred community enterprises.

A community enterprise should be understood as an activity which obtains a significant and consistent part of its income from its own trading. The importance of this strict definition has been highlighted by the experience of Amman Valley Enterprise Ltd.

based at Gwaun Cae Gurwen in West Glamorgan. Founded in 1987 this now runs five community businesses, is developing three others, and employs forty-one people, of which eleven are full-time and thirty part time.

The core of the operation is the Education and Training Department which runs more than thirty classes in co-operation with Neath College, Swansea University, West Glamorgan Community Education, the Workers' Education Association and other organisations. Subjects include Computing, Word Processing and Desk Top Publishing, Business and Finance, Women and People in Technology, Maths and English GCSE, and Welsh, German and French conversation courses.

The businesses run by Amman Valley Enterprise include Classic Catering, a community cafe which also provides for outside catering and a freezer-to-table service; Lots of Tots, a day nursery for 0-7 year-olds; Jigsaw Business Services which provide accounts and payroll, typing and word-processing, and printing and publishing services. The Amman Centre, previously Ammanford's Civic Hall, has been renovated and now operates as a private function, entertainment and conference centre. Amman Valley Enterprise's annual turnover is around £250,000 a year, of which about two-thirds is self-generated from trading. Its development officer, Maggi Dawson, emphasises the importance of the trading dimension which, she says, distinguishes community enterprise from community development:

> Trading enables you to go beyond a culture of dependency on grant aid. You have to go through a learning curve to discover the meaning and worth of enterprise from a desire to improve your community facilities. Trading generates work. It demands the discipline of thinking in terms of strategy and business plans. It increases your sense of confidence and worth if you can see the results of your efforts deriving an income. It gives you something you can measure and encourages a spirit of self-reliance. Community development is a first stage process of thinking in terms of your needs and the help you can obtain to respond to them. Community enterprise is about going beyond this, recognising your assets and responding to them with your own initiative.[18]

In statistical terms the impact of community enterprises — in total they employ perhaps 1,000 people in Wales —might be regarded as minimal. However, this disregards at least six key characteristics of community enterprises as experienced on the ground:

* Invariably the more effective community enterprises have education and training as a core element of their activity. This means that there is a continual flow of people passing through community enterprise initiatives, giving them an impact well beyond their size and number.

* More often than not community enterprises are to be found in the most disadvantaged and least well-endowed parts of the economy, both in terms of location and social class. In these locations community enterprises have usually been initiated because there was simply no alternative. They are typically to be found in areas abandoned by private enterprise and only vestigially served by public services. In these locations — sink housing estates and the run-down urban fringes of cities, coastal towns created and lost for tourism, and the more isolated Valley villages — community enterprise has proved the only way to stimulate outside interest or investment.

* Community enterprises offer the disadvantaged and least well-educated an opportunity to recover a sense of confidence and self-worth, bed-rock qualities of any enterprise culture. In tackling the enterprise problem at its root and at its most difficult, community enterprises are intervening at the base of Welsh society, thereby lifting the level of confidence of the society as a whole. In the process they are breaking down the divisions which militate against the social solidarity and co-operation which are such key features of the co-operative enterprise culture being sought.

* In a number of examples community enterprises are demonstrating that they can be a cost-effective and beneficial way of delivering key local authority services, such as care for the elderly and the disabled. The Co-options Community Co-operative, based in Rhyl, is one of the best examples in Wales. Founded in 1989 it has now developed 12 small businesses, ranging from rustic furniture and craft workshops to a mountain bicycle retail and repair business, which have provided training and work for more than 150 people with learning disabilities.

* Community enterprise is demonstrating that it can be an effective way of sustaining essential services in isolated locations, such as post offices, general stores and garages in rural villages. The village of Graig near the Clwyd-Gwynedd border is one highly successful example of a community that is being sustained in this way.

* In many localities community enterprise has proved the only means of allowing access for significant numbers of people to the arts. One notable example is Valley and Vale Community Arts, based in Barry and Blaengarw.

Community enterprise, therefore, should be seen not as a marginal and relatively insignificant activity, but one that is an essential part of generating an enterprise culture for Wales from below. If it can be effectively promoted it will provide an essential component of the key economic project for Wales in the twenty-first century: that is to say, sustainable renewal and development from within.

CREATING A CONSENSUS FOR CHANGE

Whatever area of the Welsh economy is probed in the 1990s—whether it be innovation, research and development, skills and training, the need for new investment packages, or sub-regional organisation — the accent is invariably placed on partnership and networking between the public and private sectors. Just as firms are networking to achieve mutually beneficial ends, so development agencies are trying to fashion networks to promote regional development. The rationale is very simple: regional development is becoming an ever more collective endeavour and, because no single organisation has a monopoly of wisdom, a networking approach helps to disseminate best practice to each member of the network far more rapidly than if each organisation acted alone. Networking amongst Welsh political institutions — that is to say, the interaction between the various bodies and people involved — has long been as much a part of Welsh governance as the institutions themselves.[19] This is now becoming true for the Welsh economy as well.

To assist the process we need to ensure that in future political authority more effectively and more democratically reflects our home-based tradition of partnership and co-operative endeavour. Only then can we be sure of following the Rhine model of entrepreneurial partnership. Political renewal is a prerequisite for economic renewal. We need democracy at the all-Wales level to enable us to create an appropriate entrepreneurial culture for Wales in the twenty-first century.

Wales is deeply imbued with a culture which sets a high premium on collaboration between management and labour in the economy and between the private and public sectors in general. This is a culture which will stand us in good stead in facing the task of regional economic renewal. As Kevin Morgan has put it:

> Around the world those working in Agencies concerned with regeneration have to contend with the same fundamental problem: on the one hand economic renewal is necessarily a long-term endeavour; on the other hand they must operate in such a way as to satisfy the short-term electoral cycle which is uppermost in the minds of their political masters. Where there is a strong consensus, in which politicians and officials subscribe to a broadly agreed strategy, this problem is less debilitating; where there is not, the problem can actually undermine the regional strategy itself.[20]

Wales has one advantage in agreeing a strategy. The task of absorbing lessons from elsewhere in the European Union has been rendered that much easier because the country has forged a number of alliances with such innovative Regions as Baden-Wurttemberg, Lombardy, Rhône-Alpes and Catalunya. A characteristic of all these Regions is a mature democratic structure capable of motivating their development. Being exposed to Regions with much greater institutional autonomy is a reminder that while Wales may possess a reasonable degree of institutional capacity by UK standards, it is woefully inadequate in the wider European context.

Nonetheless, it remains a paradox, not to say a contradiction, that in the face of a free-market, ideologically aligned Westminster government, Wales' institutions have managed to emulate so much of the more emollient continental patterns of partnership between the public and private sectors. With democratic self-governance driving this process forward Wales could achieve a great deal more.

NOTES

1.*Territorial Development and Structural Change: A New Perspective on Adjustment and Reform* (Paris: OECD, 1993).
2. See Philip Cooke and Kevin Morgan *The Intelligent Region*, Regional and Industrial Research Report No. 5 (Centre for Advanced Social Studies, University of Wales College of Cardiff, 1991).
3. Kevin Morgan *The Learning Region: Institutions, Innovation and Regional Renewal*, Paper in Planning Research No. 157 (Department of City and Regional Planning, University of Wales College of Cardiff, 1995).
4. Robert Putnam, 'The Prosperous Community', in *The American Prospect*, 1993.
5. 'A Survey of Wales', *The Financial Times*, August 1978.
6. *Wales 2010: Creating Our Future*, Institute of Welsh Affairs, 1993.
7. See Mark C. Cassoon, Philip Cooke, R. Merfyn Jones, Colin H. Williams, *Quiet Revolution? Language, Culture and Economy in the Nineties* (Menter a Busnes, Science Park, Aberystwyth, Dyfed SY23 3AH, 1994).
8. M. Albert, *Capitalism versus Capitalism*, 1993.
9. See Christopher Harvie, *Europe and the Welsh Nation*, Welsh Political Archive Lecture, 1994 (National Library of Wales, Aberystwyth, 1995).
10. See Kevin Morgan, 'Development from Within - Economic Renewal and a Welsh Parliament' in John Osmond (ed.) *A Parliament for Wales* (Llandysul: Gomer, 1994).
11. See John Osmond, 'A Welsh Voice in Brussels', in *Planet* No 55, February/March 1984, p. 118-120.
12. See Kevin Morgan, *The Learning Region: Institutions, Innovation and Regional Renewal* (Department of City and Regional Planning, University of Wales, Cardiff, May 1995).
13. *The Regional Technology Plan Guidebook* (Brussels: European Commission, 1994).
14. *Draft Interim Report of the Regional Technology Plan for Wales*, Welsh Development Agency, 1995. Figures compiled by the Central Statistical Office for 1994 were as follows:

	£ million	R&D Expenditure as a % of GDP
South East	5,124	2.7
East Midlands	790	2.3
South West	553	1.3
Scotland	245	0.5
North	131	0.5
Wales	113	0.4
UK (Total/Ave)	9,126	1.5

15. Welsh Development Agency *Corporate Plan 1995-6 to 1997-8*, 1995.
16. Kevin Morgan, *The Learning Region: Institutions, Innovation and Regional Renewal* op. cit.
17. The statistics listed here are contained in a paper produced by the Shadow Secretary of State for Wales, Ron Davies, *The Economic Case for a Welsh Assembly*, September 1996.
18. Interview with the author, April 1995.
19. See P.J. Madgwick and Mari James, *Government by Consultation: The Case of Wales* (Centre for the Study of Public Policy, University of Strathclyde, 1979).
20. See Kevin Morgan, 'The Fallible Servant: Making Sense of the Welsh Development Agency, Papers' in *Planning Research* No 151 (Department of City and Regional Planning, University of Wales, Cardiff, 1994).

THE FUTURE OF BROADCASTING

Welsh broadcasting has to discover its future amid a set of global and local contradictions. De-regulation and the growth of new multi-media technologies are accelerating the globalisation of the industry. At the same time these trends carry the danger of cutting viewers and listeners off from a knowable and actually lived experience. Broadcasting can promote, but it can also destroy local roots.

Where does Wales and territorial Welsh broadcasting fit into the global footprints of satellite transmission? The answer lies partly in a paradox. For while broadcasting, like the economy in which it swims, is now a global phenomenon, both are increasingly finding their roots in a regional space. The term region is, of course, disputed. Wales has never had a state, or only fleetingly in medieval times, and so lacks many of the trappings of statehood. Yet we are still a nation in some sense of that term. In the Introduction it was suggested that a way of describing our situation was that we are a people struggling to become a nation by progressively establishing our own institutions. In this project broadcasting, and the Welsh broadcasting institutions that are presently evolving, have a pivotal and hence highly political role.

The ambiguity at the centre of the argument is reflected in the BBC's own terminology which refers to Wales, along with Scotland and Northern Ireland, as a National Region. Therein lies a central paradox or contradiction at the heart of British broadcasting. Inside it, however, rests the potential for advance. We retain in Wales a strong sense of our own identity, however that is defined, and that is reflected by the 'actually existing' broadcasting institutions and their relative autonomy — S4C and the wave of independent producers that have grown up in its wake, BBC Wales, and HTV Wales.

The struggle for autonomy is taking place within an affirmative European context. Across both Eastern and Western Europe a variety of regional and national identities are surviving, and sometimes thriving, despite the increasingly global characteristics of the economy and broadcasting environment. The regional and global dimensions are but two sides of the same coin, with the older nation-state structure being compressed inbetween.

Wales confronts a particular dimension of this European broadcasting experience because of the presence of two native languages with, paradoxically, the weaker being the stronger in specifically Welsh broadcasting terms. This has led, naturally, to demands being made on behalf of English language broadcasting, both from outside the system and increasingly from within. Just as the politics of devolution sets up a whole range of tensions and struggles between establishments, so the demand for a more comprehensive Welsh broadcasting service in English sets up equivalent tensions in the broadcasting milieu. In the mid-1990s a struggle is underway inside the BBC, with the centralists in London having to deal with increasingly pressing demands from the 'regions', mainly Wales and Scotland. In this the Welsh agenda is clear. It was stated unequivocally by the present controller of BBC Wales, Geraint Talfan Davies, at the start of the decade:

> There is a problem. About 85 per cent of our present eight hours a week of English output is news, current affairs, and sport, that is reactive programming, or topical programming geared to specific events. That leaves only 15 per cent to reflect upon every other aspect of Welsh life and it is not good enough. We have to find more hours for English language programming so that we can provide a more complete reflection of the political, economic, cultural and artistic life of Wales.[1]

THE BATTLE FOR RESOURCES

Since this declaration in 1990, the number of hours of English language-programmes transmitted by BBC Wales on BBC 1 and BBC 2 have crept up from eight to between ten and eleven per week. This has had an impact on HTV Wales which, under the pressure of the renewal of its franchise in the early 1990s, reached a similar level. But this small increase has made a minimal impact on the 'problem' that the BBC Wales Controller identified. The point is well illustrated by comparing the rounded S4C Welsh language service offered to the fifth or so of the population who can understand it.

It is difficult to overestimate the importance of the establishment of S4C in 1982, not just in increasing the quantity and range of Welsh language broadcasting, but as an institution in itself. Both are providing benchmarks against which provision in the English language is being judged.

BBC Wales supplies around ten hours-a-week peak-time Welsh-language programmes to S4C, a third of the channel's Wales-produced output. BBC Wales transmits around the same number of hours a week in English on BBC 1 and BBC 2 — much of it, however, apart from the nightly early-evening news, at non-peak hours. For a fifth of the Welsh population BBC Wales was spending £17.6m on programmes in 1995-6, and for the remaining four-fifths of the English-speaking Welsh population £15.3m.

At the same time there is a large imbalance in the programmes being supplied by BBC Wales for network transmission. The combined populations of Wales, Scotland and Northern Ireland comprise about 17% of the UK population. Together they supply just 3% of UK network television production. Wales supplies between 15 and 30 hours a year, that is between 0.2% and 0.4%. Over the first half of the 1990s Wales contribution within this range has been reducing. So, in 1993-4 BBC Wales contributed 23 hours of network programming, compared with 71 hours in 1990-91.

If Wales was allowed to contribute network programming on the basis of its proportion of the United Kingdom population — that is, five per cent — funding and production of Welsh-based programming would be increased by a factor of at least ten. On grounds of fairness alone this is not an unreasonable aspiration. It is certainly shared by broadcasters in Scotland. The fact that, viewed from London, such demands are regarded as impractical, not to say unreasonable, is another indication of the contradictions lurking at the heart of Welsh broadcasting. BBC Wales sees no contradiction between improving its local service while at the same time linking up with the emerging global patterns of broadcasting. The BBC in London might acknowledge the case, but will not allow the air time or the resources to allow it to happen.

One reason is the innate metropolitan, actually parochial, character of the BBC as an organisation. In 1994 it announced that an extra £75 million would be allocated to the regions on a competitive basis over the next four years. Cardiff, for instance, was designated a 'centre of excellence' for music and a promise was made of more funding for drama productions. Yet in practice this has not resulted in more hours or resources for Welsh broadcasting on the network schedules. Instead, there has been a heightened battle for resources, with BBC Wales at best holding the line against the undermining of its resource base. It is not a platform from which a significantly improved service for English-speaking viewers in Wales can be easily built.

The battle for resources is, of course, not new. It has been going on for decades, as the former BBC Wales Controller Gareth Price has testified. The fact that it seems to have been institutionalised to Wales' disadvantage compared, not just with London but other parts of the BBC system, suggests that a political shift in a democratic direction will be required to achieve any fundamental change. The main issue, says Gareth Price, is an attitude of condescension on the part of London management:

> All (BBC Wales) Controllers have suffered from this syndrome in the battles with Network Controllers. Bill Cotton, then Managing Director of BBC TV, once attempted to do a deal with me in Llandaff itself — 'You do Rugby Special for us and forget all other network programmes'. Their unspoken reasons for such negative attitudes are simple. Untidy Network Controllers such as Aubrey Singer could be mavericks and commission a costly series such as *The Life and Times of David Lloyd George* from Wales only if they found the money from London departments which depended on a continuing annual budget for their livelihood. Wales was never designated a Network Centre as was Scotland and Bristol. Wales was a nuisance where lorry loads of money crossed the Severn Bridge to maintain a minority channel which was a political sop to the Nationalists. These are the perceptions which continue to govern the thinking of most BBC London executives in private even today.[2]

SELF-DEFEATING COMPETITION

Meanwhile HTV, the other main broadcaster in Wales, is hamstrung in producing home-produced programmes by the commercial pressures on its channel combined with the ludicrously unfair levy it is forced to pay the Treasury for its broadcasting franchise. The 1990 Broadcasting Act penalised Wales more than most parts of the ITV network. HTV paid £20.3 million for the right to broadcast to the people of Wales and the West of England. This compared with a bid of £2,000 each made by Scottish and Central Television where there was not the same competition from aspirant franchise-holders.

The £1.75 million cheque that HTV pays to the Treasury each month is, in effect, a gratuitous broadcasting tax on the people of Wales. The result has been retrenchment, job cuts, slashed programme budgets, and a pushing of Wales-produced material to the far corners of the schedule where it will be little noticed by the advertisers nor, for the most part, by the viewers.

The main peak-time output of both BBC Wales and HTV Wales is news programmes. Yet these operate in such a competitive environment that the main half-hour daily news programmes, BBC's *Wales Today* and HTV's *Wales Tonight* are now both transmitted at the same time: 6.30pm. The result of this aggressively competitive move, by HTV in March 1994, was simply to lower the combined reach of the two programmes. Before the change *Wales Today* had an audience of about 326,000 viewers and HTV's news programme, transmitted half-an-hour earlier, around 298,000. When HTV moved its slot it had the advantage of inheriting viewers from an Australian soap opera scheduled immediately beforehand. This had the result of securing the audience for its revamped *Wales Tonight*, modelled closely on *Wales Today*. However, the BBC's *Wales Today* audience fell back to 281,000. The immediate overall audience loss, therefore, was 45,000 viewers.[3] Since then the figures have fluctuated. Some weeks BBC Wales is ahead, other weeks HTV Wales. What is not in doubt is that it is the viewers that have lost. They have less choice and overall the total number watching the Welsh early evening news has fallen.

Such self-defeating competition has led to the question whether the duplication can be justified. There is, of course, an argument that on liberal democratic principle, it is necessary to have at least two television sources for Welsh news and current affairs. On the other hand, with such a minimal range of home-produced English language output can we afford it? If there was co-operation across the English language airwaves, as happens with the Welsh language service on S4C, existing resources could be released for other and more varied programme strands.

English language viewers in Wales could have one nightly news programme instead of two, one current affairs programme a week instead of two, one environment programme instead of two, and one weekly sports magazine programme instead of two. With sensitive scheduling between the channels up to four more hours of other programmes could be created for the English language audience utilising existing resources. That such an initiative is unlikely in present circumstances is another indication that a political shift in a democratic direction will be necessary before progressive change can occur.

THE SEARCH FOR A DISTINCTIVE IMAGE

In the wake of the damaging effort to retain its franchise, HTV's strategy for improving its programmes has been to start by rebuilding the financial base and strength of its organisation. In 1994 its share of total ITV advertising revenue was 6.1%, representing an income of £91.2 million and pre-tax profits of £7.3 million. This turnaround in financial fortunes was achieved in part by collaboration with other companies, for instance the Flextech cable and media group which took a 20 per cent share in HTV in 1994. A merger with Scottish Television is another possibility. HTV is also extending its business beyond programmes to include publishing and merchandising. At the same time it is actively pursuing access to other channels and media. For instance, in early 1995 it joined a consortium including Virgin Communications and Associated Newspapers to bid for the Channel 5 broadcasting licence.[4] However, whether all this activity will result in improved and better scheduled Welsh programming remains far from clear.

During 1994 HTV Wales broadcast an average of just over 11 hours a week, which was 39 minutes above the licence requirement. However, fewer programmes were supplied to the network than in 1993. The programmes that did reach the network were generally products from the West of England part of the HTV dual region. These were the drama serials *Wyecliffe* and *Poldark*, and childrens' programmes such as *Budgie, the Little Helicopter* and *The Famous Five*. This concentration on English rather than Welsh material for network programming is another, clear indication that network schedulers have a disinclination to commission programmes from Wales. HTV is also increasingly making programmes for other outlets, including cable television and satellite channels such as UK Living, the Children's Channel, and the Learning, Family, and Discovery Channels.

BBC Wales' future plans remaining attached to securing improved access to network programming. 'We are very, very determined to get drama on the network,' said BBC Wales's head of English language programmes, Dai Smith, in the summer of 1995.[5] If achieved this would have the triple advantage of increasing the number of English language programmes for and about Wales, of projecting Wales to the wider world, and of improving budgets for Welsh programme makers.

Desirable as they are, there is a distinct problem in attaining these objectives. For, as we have seen, there is a lack of commitment, let alone enthusiasm from the controllers of BBC 1 and BBC 2 towards commissioning Welsh programmes. There is no dispute that this tendency worsened in the first half of the 1990s. And there is little evidence that, in a less favourable financial position in the later 1990s, the position is likely to change a great deal.

One BBC Wales response has been to try and create a product it thinks the market will tolerate. So, for example, faced with the lack of enthusiasm in London for Welsh-produced drama, or certainly drama that has a strong Welsh character or unambiguously Welsh themes, it has sought to produce programmes which contain minimal reference to Wales. The result has been such offerings as the five-part drama series *Oliver's Travels*, transmitted by BBC 1 in the summer of 1995, in a peak-time Sunday evening slot. This series had an English writer Alan Plater and an English lead actor Alan Bates. The story was about an eccentric English academic made redundant from the University of Glamorgan going off in search of a crossword compiler known as Aristotle. The locations began in the Welsh Valleys but led quickly after the first episode to the English Midlands and then the Orkneys.

It was a whimsical tale, a mixture of murder and love story, with the Irish actress Sinead Cusack playing opposite Alan Bates. It was well produced, and attracted a good audience. One was left wondering, however, why it was made by BBC Wales. Beyond being entertainment, what messages was it giving Welsh viewers? What kind of Wales was it projecting to the wider UK audience?

These are complex questions that tread a fine line between

parochialism and narrow exclusivity on the one hand, and the search for a particularity of place, accent and experience that nonetheless contain universal messages on the other. S4C has less of a problem in this regard. Any dramatic theme, however cosmopolitan, is immediately inflected with a Welsh perspective, merely by it being expressed through the medium of the Welsh language. By the same token writers, producers and actors for S4C, with very few exceptions, are assured of a Welsh background. The same, of course, is not true when it comes to producing Welsh programmes in English even though 'English is a Welsh language'.

In this the Welsh language creates a particular dilemma for English-speaking Welsh people. On one side of them is the appealing mass of English/American culture channelled overwhelmingly through centralised London-based television; on the other is a vivid, if less powerful, Welsh language culture channelled through S4C. There are, as a result, at least two entirely separate arenas for communication within Wales — and three if you divide the English language audience between those who point their television aerials towards English-based transmitters and those who tune in to BBC Wales and HTV Wales.

Wales is expert at living inside such contradictions. What it tends to induce, however, is uncertainty, disunity, a fractured image of the self, and most fundamentally a lack of cultural confidence. For a combination of reasons, to do with history and notions of Britishness and Welshness tied into linguistic dilemmas, Wales seems more prone to fundamental lack of cultural self-confidence than Scotland. This must be part of the background explanation why, though Scotland and even Northern Ireland have succeeded in producing television drama that is uncompromisingly Scottish and Irish, Wales has found it much harder to find an equivalent expression.

Broadcasting is an inextricable part of the problem of a lack of cultural confidence — and the 'culture of defeat' explored in Chapter 10 — that afflicts contemporary Welshness. Broadcasting must necessarily, therefore, be part of the solution.

THE SPECIAL RESPONSIBILITY OF BBC WALES

Broadcasting in Wales has to operate in an environment where there is a lack of other media provision. In contrast with

Scotland, serious newspaper journalism in Wales is weak. The two daily morning newspapers — the *Western Mail* and the *Daily Post* now owned by the same group — fail to provide a comprehensive, let alone fully geographic national perspective on Welsh affairs.

Around 90 per cent of Welsh newspaper readers buy papers emanating from London in which the Welsh dimension of the news is vestigial. This is in a situation where most domestic spending and provision of services — and a budget of £6.5 billion in 1995-6 — is within the purview of the Welsh Office. All this places a special responsibility on the broadcasters, and specially BBC Wales since HTV Wales fails to penetrate large areas of north and north-eastern Wales.

This responsibility has been publicly recognised by BBC Wales itself. During 1992-3 it held more than fifty public consultations seeking views on how it should prepare for its Charter renewal in 1996. In a presentation to the Assembly of Welsh Counties towards the end of this effort it summarised its strategic objectives, saying that BBC Wales radio and television should:

> * Guarantee the national debate, principally by news and current affairs programming
>
> * Highlight the sporting, ceremonial and artistic events that galvanise the nation of Wales
>
> * Nurture — as well as reflect — excellence and innovation in the arts and entertainment
>
> * Serve the needs of Wales as a learning society
>
> * Iluminate regional diversity within Wales
>
> * Provide, in short, the social glue that binds all the communities of Wales together.[6]

This is an ambitious 'mission statement'. Yet given BBC Wales' static financial position and lack of access to network programming, it sounded more like a series of aspirations than a potential reality to the councillors from throughout Wales who listened to a presentation based on it in early 1993. In response they passed a stern resolution calling for: an immediate increase in the number of English-language television programmes produced by BBC Wales; the reversal of the centralisation of decision-making and resources away from BBC Wales to London; and for the role of the Broadcasting Council for Wales, the appointed body that theoretically controls 'programme policy and content', to be enhanced.[7]

AN ENGLISH LANGUAGE CHANNEL

Against the background of mounting demand for an increased range of locally-produced programmes in Wales — demonstrated once more in 1995 by resolutions passed at the Wales TUC and Wales Labour Party conferences — it is instructive to look at what the Welsh Language Board said in 1989. This was in response to the Government's White Paper on Broadcasting in the 1990s: *Competition, Choice and Quality*, produced prior to the legislation that established ITV's Channel 3:

> Increasingly, a nation is becoming what television says it is. People's perceptions of themselves are developed through these external influences rather than through personal and shared experiences. For Wales these external influences are more likely to come from Los Angeles and London than they are to come from Cardiff and they threaten the sense of being Welsh and therefore the long-term survival of the Welsh language...
>
> Any plan for safeguarding Welsh broadcasting must cater equally for the interests of Welsh-speakers and non-Welsh-speakers. The language may be a manifestation of our separate culture as Welsh people or it may be one end result of other deep-rooted differences.
>
> Whatever the truth, the language cannot survive in a nation where non-Welsh-speakers do not continue to feel themselves to be different from the other people of the United Kingdom. Television is the prime influence in creating the cultural climate which can nurture or destroy those differences.[8]

The Welsh Language Board went on to press the case for equivalent treatment for the English language on television within Wales as the Welsh. This, it argued, could only mean the setting up of an English-language channel for Wales along similar lines to S4C. A question that follows is the extent to which that aspiration is shared by the English-speaking Welsh themselves.

The only hard evidence — a poll conducted by the *Western Mail* in February 1990 — indicates strong support. The response to the question 'Would you be in favour of Wales having its own television channel to serve English speakers in the same way that S4C serves Welsh speakers?' was:

	%
In favour	73
Against	17
Don't Know	11

Of course, the question was in one sense superficial in that it did not make it clear that the creation of such a channel, with more home-originated programmes at peak hours, would at that time have resulted in a deprivation effect. That is to say, Welsh viewers would be deprived to some extent of programmes coming from London, though depending on the precise arrangements that were made for an English-language channel, such programmes could be re-scheduled in the same way that Channel 4 UK programmes are re-scheduled on S4C.

Whatever the strength of such arguments — and, as we shall see, digital television technology is providing an answer — it is plain that there is a strong inter-relationship between the Welsh and English languages in the development of television in Wales. Such improvements to the English language service that have occurred, certainly during the 1980s, did so in response to the advances made in Welsh-language television.

Equally, as the Welsh Language Board has made clear, safeguarding those advances now requires a much improved and more stable environment for English-language television. At the time of its intervention, in 1989, the Board made the case for using ITV's Channel 3 as the basis for a dedicated English language Channel for Wales, with BBC Wales contributing its programme to it instead of transmitting them on BBC 1 and BBC 2. However, with Channel 3 now well established and HTV more of a commercial than a public service broadcaster, this is unlikely to be a serious prospect.

As it has itself recognised, only BBC Wales can now guarantee a truly national platform for debate in both languages and across both television and radio. It is the only broadcaster in Wales that can claim to be national — geographically covering the whole of Wales — and the only one that claims to be both a cultural patron and provider of a range of quality programme services.

An indication that the debate had moved on in this direction came from the Celtic Film and Television Association in 1993 when it called for BBC 2 to become a decentralised opt-out service and the basis, in Wales, for a dedicated English-language channel capable of providing an integrated home station to match S4C. The Association was reacting to the Government's 1992 Green Paper on the future of the BBC and the BBC's own response *Extending Choice*. In particular, it drew attention to a marked difference between the two documents in the way they articulated concern for Scotland, Wales and Northern Ireland:

> The Green Paper takes an open-minded view of the needs and expectations of audiences outwith London and the English regions. *Extending Choice* subordinates national broadcasting in the nations of the UK into a regional structure and pays scant attention to the linguistic and cultural needs of the UK nations...
>
> It is assumed, almost imperialistically, that the nations of these islands, known somewhat euphemistically as 'National Regions' by the BBC, are 'special interest' groups who need separate consideration. This kind of quasi-District Commissioner view of the Celtic fringe seems out of step with the cultural and institutional devolution which is taking place, both in the British and European context.
>
> It may be difficult sometimes for a large London-based monolithic organisation to comprehend that the centre of the world to people living in Wales, is Wales, and that the view of the world follows the lines that emanate from the living culture of an ancient nation. It is a profound error to indulge in institutional tokenism when considering programmes and services in the Celtic countries. Things do not always fall apart because the centre cannot hold.[9]

A MEDIUM-TERM STRATEGY

It is unlikely that without political pressure, of the kind that would come with the creation of devolved political institition for Wales, that the BBC in London would contemplate the branding of either BBC 2 or BBC 1 as an autonomous BBC Wales with increased home-produced programming and, crucially, autonomous scheduling. It is inevitable, however, that once devolution occurs, pressure will mount for this to happen or for some other way to be found to provide a dedicated, autonomous English language television service for Wales to match S4C.

Meanwhile, there are available a range of medium-term policies for improving the service. One would be to increase the present 10-11 hours -a-week programming to around 18-20 hours a week, as has been advocated by the Welsh Campaign for Quality Television.[10] This could involve a significant addition of high-quality drama and documentary strands. More fundamentally —from the point of view of the BBC viewed as a self-consciously *British* organisation — it could entail a restructuring of the early evening news scheduling, between 6pm and 7pm.

In alliance with BBC Scotland, BBC Wales is pressing the case for an abolition of the London-produced 6 o'clock news and merging it with the 6.30pm 'regional' news programme into an hour-long integrated news service. This would provide Wales and Scotland with a programme in which international, British and Welsh/Scottish 'national/regional' news were woven together.

The project is very much a drawing board aspiration and is being fiercely resisted by the BBC in London. Yet the fact that a case for it is being made at all represents an important shift in the approach of BBC Wales and BBC Scotland. The arguments being mounted from both countries include:

> * London-based news programmes contain too many items that have only limited relevance to Wales and Scotland.
>
> * The initiative would enhance the staus of Welsh and Scottish journalism and provide a broader context in which the Welsh and Scottish audiences could consider their own particular news agendas.
>
> * It would be an opportunity for the BBC as a whole to demonstrate its commitment to the the diversity of the United Kingdom, as laid down in its own document *Extending Choice.*
>
> * The developing European dimension of Welsh and Scottish affairs now requires a changed structure along these lines.
>
> * In the context of European broadcasting such an

> approach would mean that BBC Wales and BBC Scotland would join the mainstream in their approach to news gathering and transmission. It would be an acknowledgement that the world of broadcasting is at one and the same time moving in more global and more local directions.

THE BROADCASTING REVOLUTION

Such are some of the arguments for improvements to the Welsh broadcasting system in the medium-term. At the same time new broadcasting technology is changing the terms of the argument so far as providing a completely new and dedicated English language channel for Wales is concerned. An English language channel for Wales, additional to the existing channels, is now on the agenda because of the imminent digital broadcasting revolution. The immediate impact, before the end of the 1990s, will be a quadrupling of the capacity of the present four UK terrestrial channels. When added to new capacity on satellite as many as eighteen entirely new channels will be created.[11]

The timing of the introduction of the new channels and precisely how they will be allocated amongst the broadcasters, remains unclear. One estimate is that digital broadcasting will be introduced sometime in the period between 1998 and 2000. As to the allocation of the new channels, as always that will be subject to political pressure. Channel 4, for instance, has already made it clear that its first priority in Wales will be to see that itself and S4C are broadcast on two separate digitised channels.

The time-scale for the introduction of digital television neatly coincides with Labour's plans of introducing a Welsh Assembly. There is no doubt that an Assembly will want to have a say, and will certainly bring much influence to bear, on the structure of Welsh broadcasting. Dominated as it inevitably will by English-speaking members, the Assembly will want equivalent provision for English as for Welsh language broadcasting in Wales. It is likely to object strongly to the £20.3 million a year levy paid by HTV to the Whitehall Treasury, as an arbitrary extra broadcasting tax on the Welsh people. This could well be re-negotiated, if not abolished, but in return perhaps for guarantees of programme participation by HTV Wales in a new digitised English language Channel for Wales.

BBC Wales' relationship with S4C is likely to be re-examined. There could well be a merger between the two organisations, to reduce administrative overhead costs — by as much as £5 million a year. There will also be calls to bring both BBC Wales and S4C under the aegis of a new Welsh Broadcasting Authority responsible for the separate Welsh and English language radio and television channels. In any event, S4C is likely to suggest being given the right to re-broadcast BBC opt-outs as a *quid pro quo* for Channel 4 spreading to Wales.

For cultures such as Wales broadcasting offers both opportunities and threats. It can promote all the things BBC Wales has called for in statements such as the one it made to the Assembly of Welsh Counties in 1993. It can guarantee national debate, nurture excellence and innovation in the arts and entertainment, promote regional diversity within Wales, and at the same time provide 'the social glue that binds all of the communities of Wales together'. But it can only achieve these objectives if it has the appropriate structures, finances and autonomy. Without them Welsh broadcasting will be part of a destructive global force, centralising culture and denying autonomy. In that process the potential for Welsh comunities and the individuals within them to feel a sense of belonging and nurture a connected sense of responsibility, will be undermined.

This is what what is at stake in the broadcasting revolution that confronts Wales in the next decade. There could be no more profound statement of the need for democratic institutions within which that revolution can be steered to best suit our own very specific, and very special, broadcasting and cultural needs.

NOTES

1. *See for Yourself*, BBC Wales (Cardiff) 7 January 1991.
2. Gareth Price, review of John Davies, *Broadcasting and the BBC in Wales*, University of Wales Press, 1995, in *New Welsh Review*, No.29, Summer 1995, p.78.
3. Both BBC Wales and HTV Wales are reluctant to reveal viewing figures such as these, which are regarded as commercially sensitive. These statistics have been obtained from internal sources.
4. 'Rising star HTV has galactic ambitions', *Western Mail*, 12 July 1995.

5. 'Emphasis on the laughs as BBC Wales denies ducking Yentob challenge', *Western Mail*, 24 August 1995. The report noted that the controller of BBC 2, Alan Yentob had cricised BBC Wales for failing to produce a successful serial drama for the network. Only one of BBC Wales' twenty-eight programmes being unveiled for the 1995 Autumn season was a drama — Karl Francis' *Streetlife*, a tale of an unmarried mothers' struggle to survive in the Valleys.
6. *The Role of BBC Wales*, report to the Asembly of Welsh Counties, April 1993.
7. See John Osmond, 'The Last Output of Imperialism: The Future of the Broadcasting Council for Wales', *Planet* No. 99, June 1993.
8. Welsh Language Board, Letter to Rt. Hon. Peter Walker MP, Secretary of State for Wales, 7 March 1989.
9. *The Future of the BBC: A Response to the Government Green Paper*, The Celtic Film and Television Association, April 1993.
10. *Power To Choose: The Future of the BBC in Wales*, Campaign for Quality Television, April 1993.
11. See the White Paper on Digital Broadcasting, August 1995. Digital television and radio involves converting sound and pictures into computer language which can be transmitted in compressed form. Signals are received and decoded by a set-top black box. The technology opens the way for cinema-style wide screen television and CD quality sound.

UNITARY BRITAIN AND REGIONAL EUROPE

Britain and Europe are two arenas that compete for attention when assessing Wales' place in the world. Increasingly, however, a third, world-wide dimension has to be taken into account. In the 1990s the global economy is undermining the British nation-state as much as Wales and Scotland or the European Union. By the global economy is meant the dominance of multinational companies together with the ever-growing, world-wide nexus of communication and currency movements. Together they are fatally undermining nation-state power and sovereignty. One response is a movement throughout the world towards continental patterns of governance. In our own case this last is represented by the evolving institutions of the European Union. At the same time parallel Regional structures, below the nation-state, are emerging as well. In combination the continental and Regional levels of governance have some hope of subjecting global economic and cultural forces to democratic discipline.

It is the nation-state, of course, that from this perspective remains the problem. Part of the confusion that results from this analysis is the question of nationalism. There are, in fact two kinds of nationalism involved — big nation-state nationalism, and small-nation nationalism of the kind found in Wales and Scotland. In the 1990s the latter is no longer confined to the nationalist parties in these countries. Increasingly it is to be found within wings of the other progressive parties as well, Labour, the Liberal Democrats, and even some elements of the Green parties. In Wales it is represented by a small-nation nationalist grouping that emerged inside the Welsh Labour Party in the mid-1990s. Aligning itself with a similar pressure group that appeared on the Scottish scene in the mid-1980s, it calls itself Welsh Labour Action and is campaigning for an Assembly 'with real power'.[1]

Distinctions within the unitary British state between small and big-nation nationalism (perhaps characterised by a lower-case n and an upper-case N) are important. Raymond Williams constantly emphasised it, for instance in an interview in 1984:

> There are two kinds of nationalism. There is that nationalism which reinforces the idea of the traditional nation-state. This nationalism has been given added impetus under the Thatcher governments as we saw at the time of the Falklands/Malvinas episode. But this kind of nationalism is also shared by the Labour Party, as was so vividly revealed by their support for the British intervention in the South Atlantic. The other kind of nationalism is that which questions the whole basis of the unitary British state. I think that the first kind of nationalism is reactionary and the second is progressive. This argument starts from the analysis that existing nation-states of the size of Britain are both too small and too large for useful politics.[2]

Taking this analysis forward what does being a small 'n' Welsh nationalist mean in the mid-1990s? Reiterating the view of Saunders Lewis, in his 1926 lecture *The Princples of Nationalism*, it is to say that Wales does not wish for an independent sovereign state on the nineteenth century pattern. Instead, it seeks a place for a relatively autonomous country within the framework of a European Union of the Regions. Both the Nation-State and Regionalist positions outlined here face dilemmas. Those who seek to promote the nation-state confront Raymond Williams' analysis, a reactionary cul de sac down which the Europhobic English nationalists within Conservative Party are travelling. Equally, however, the Regionalist approach contains many problems.

A starting point in tackling these questions is to examine some of the arguments that were deployed during the 1970s when devolution politics were last an important question for British politics. The Labour Government of that decade not only wrestled with Wales and Scotland, but with the Regions of England as well, though as something of an afterthought. Concern with England was prompted by Tam Dalyell's West Lothian Question[3] and the growing mutterings of a revolt from Labour MPs in the North of England.

By way of a response the Government produced, in December 1976, a document seeking to discover, as it put it, 'ways people in England would like to see our institutions develop'.[4] The press hand-out that accompanied it said a thousand bodies across England were being consulted. We never heard the outcome of that investigation. Indeed, the document *Devolution: The English*

Dimension was quickly forgotten at the time and has not been resurrected since.

Reading it today there is a sense of perspectives having changed a great deal in a relatively short period. The document made no specific proposals but rehearsed some of the arguments in favour, and against, regional government in England. The case for change was seen to be:

1. Lightening the burden on central government.
2. Bringing government close to the people.
3. Rendering the work of nominated bodies — that is, the Quangos — subject to local democratic control.
4. Providing a layer of government to deal with matters — such as planning, infrastructure, water and health — at an intermediate level between central and local government.

Arguments against change were:

1. Constitutional implications, in particular the powers of Ministers to maintain national policies, and the role of Parliament.
2. Financial implications.
3. The problem of drawing boundaries.
4. Effects on other institutions, especially the possibility of drawing functions away from local government when it had only just been reorganised.

The constitutional implications were seen as the most serious, though it is interesting that no mention was made of the West Lothian Question and the potential for English regional devolution to address this. More generally, the whole tenor of the devolution proposals in the 1970s as revealed here — for Scotland and Wales as much as for England — emphasised the economic primacy of Whitehall. Devolution was seen as involving essentially social policy matters. Economic policy — including regional policy, development grants, and public investment — were to remain firmly with central government. The paper emphasises several times the economic unity of the United Kingdom which it said, had many important aspects including:

> ... not only external economic relations, the management of demand in the United Kingdom as a whole and the framework of trade, but also the task of devising national policies to benefit particular parts of the United Kingdom and of distributing resources among them according to relative need.

The conclusion was unambiguous: 'The Government will retain direct control over economic management and over regional policy and commercial policy.'

CHANGE IN THE 1980S

The 1979 general election which was precipitated by the devolution referendums in Scotland and Wales, marked a watershed. The incoming Conservative government was highly centralist. It launched a sustained attack on local government including rate capping, imposition of the poll-tax, and the abolition of the Greater London Council and the other English metropolitan authorities. Notions of regionalism were also given short shrift. The Regional Economic Planning Councils, established in the mid-1960s, were abolished in 1981.

At the same time the 1980s saw the beginnings of an intellectual transformation in Labour thinking towards economic planning and the central state. In 1982 a Labour Working Group, headed by John Prescott, then spokesman on Regional Affairs and Devolution, published a radical paper in light of previous thinking, *Alternative Regional Strategy*. This argued against Whitehall centralism and made the case for economic regeneration from the bottom up, by building new economic and financial institutions in the regions of England as well as in Wales and Scotland, and making them democratically accountable.[5]

Such thinking was further developed through the 1980s, with the European dimension adding significantly to the argument. In 1988, for instance, Sheffield MP Richard Caborne, then Labour's Parliamentary spokesman for the Regions, published a paper entitled *Regional Renaissance: Meeting the Challenge in Europe*. This contained the following statement:

> In the past regional initiatives have concentrated on attracting inward investment. Whilst this is to be

> encouraged, experience has shown that the low skill, branch plant economy associated with this type of investment is the first victim of recession. A successful policy must therefore combine the instruments of regional policy with policies that focus on strengthening the indigenous economy in all the regions...
>
> Equally important, a new regional policy must shift the focus of decision-making to the regions. Not only is this in the interests of greater democracy and accountability, it is also the means of establishing a better balance in the economy and the basis for more sustained growth throughout the country.

While such fresh thinking — heavily influenced by the European regional dimension — was beginning to emerge on the Left during the 1980s, something similar was happening, if not on the mainstream political Right then certainly in the realm of business and trade. During the 1980s mechanisms for allocating the European Regional Development Fund and subsequently Structural Fund moneys through the 'programme approach' resulted in pressure from the European Union on what had previously been considered domestic concerns. So, for instance, the Commission began to insist on the production of detailed regional programmes, based on 'partnerships' between the various public and private agencies involved in economic development.

The launching of the Single European Market, the European Economic Area and further enlargement of the Union heightened awareness of the opportunities and competitive threats of a trading bloc of some 380 million people. Business leaders in Britain became increasingly concerned about the weakness of the business support infrastructure in the English Regions, compared with comparable areas on continental Europe.

A landmark study on the economic development lessons that needed to be absorbed was published in 1992 by the organisation Business in the Community together with Coopers and Lybrand. 'We believe within the UK there is a lack of recognition of the increasing threat that the full extent of inter-regional European competition represents,' the study declared.[6] It examined four contrasting European Regions — Catalunya, Limburg in the Netherlands, Lombardy and Hamburg and noted that each contained powerful economic development bodies at a scale and with sufficient autonomy to achieve 'critical mass'. As a result they could:

> 1. Raise and apply resources from within their region.
>
> 2. Take decisions.
>
> 3. Implement a European/international strategy at a scale which enables the region to compete effectively against other locations.

This idea of 'critical mass' was a keynote conclusion, and provides a useful additional identity marker in the continuing debate over what should constitute a definition or description of a Region in the European context:

> 'Critical mass' is likely to differ from area to area, for example our study areas ranged from 1 to 8-9 million people, but the key factors are that economic development covers a geographic area for which there exists a shared identity, with the result that common development needs and objectives can be established; that all relevant public and private organisations in the area can be and are involved in formulating and implementing strategy; that economies of scale in research, marketing and administration are facilitated; that liaison with UK government and with the EC is effective; and that a sufficient level of skills and resources is available to offer a broad range of high quality support services.

THE INTEGRATED REGIONAL OFFICES

It was against the background of pressure such as this that the Conservative Party manifesto at the 1992 general election made a commitment to the introduction of Integrated Regional Offices. In April 1994 the Departments of Trade and Industry, Employment, Environment and Transport were combined into ten new regional offices — for London, the South East, the South West, East Anglia, the East Midlands, the West Midlands, Yorkshire and Humberside, the North West, the North-East, and Merseyside. The result is that an embryo government administration for the Regions in England has been put in place.

The new offices are each responsible for administering a single geographical area They are responsible for administering or advising on £6 billion of public spending. They also administer the newly integrated programme for inner-city regeneration, the Single Regeneration Budget, combining twenty separate programmes, worth initially £1.4 billion. For the first time 2,800 staff from four different ministries in the Regions are all accountable to one Senior Regional Director. The combined running costs add up to £90 million.[7]

This process is precisely what occurred in Wales under the Macmillan government in 1962-3 and was the direct precursor of the establishment of the Welsh Office in 1964. The precedent is clear, though initially at least the new English Regional Offices and their directors smack of the old French Prefectorial system. Their operation soon attracted the attention of MPs in these terms. Peter Kilfoyle, Labour MP for Liverpool Walton, complained to the Public Accounts Committee:

> I cannot even discover how the structure works, who gives the final nod. The system seems to be running secretively, with grants of up to £3.8 million awarded without any elected representative considering the application. The regional director seems the most powerful influence in the process. He has extra powers which lead me to think of him as a viceroy appointed by a faraway power, with little or no regard for local opinion or democratic rights. Is this network of civil servants and Quangocrats giving value for money or is their function more political in nature?[8]

Quite apart from this structure other government departments and Quangos, including the NHS, have a strong presence at the regional level in England. English Quangos now spend an estimated £50 billion a year, with much of the spending — around £30 billion from higher and further education, urban regeneration and housing — transferred from local government. The Prime Minister, John Major, revealed that in the South-West alone there were forty-three different regional outposts of central government employing 26,000 people.[9]

Although the new Integrated Regional Offices are tightly controlled by the civil service, their creation did not occur without opposition and a Whitehall rearguard action. There was a hard-fought Cabinet debate despite the manifesto commitment, with John Major holding out against the change, which was supported by Michael Heseltine, President of the Board of Trade, and Kenneth Clarke, the Chancellor of the Exchequer. Heseltine and Clarke, reflecting Conservative business pressure, made the case on grounds of efficiency. Major, it seems, was worried about the political implications of institutionalising the English regions on such firm economic foundations.

Major was right. His view was cofirmed, if in a backhanded way, by Howard Davies, speaking in February 1995 when he was still Director-general of the CBI (shortly before becoming Deputy Governor of the Bank of England):

> There is a growing consensus that a regional focus for decision-making across the public sector needs to be created, and one with business input ... Regional businesses have definitely welcomed having a single point of call for government in their region. But curiously rather than appease the enthusiasm for regional autonomy, and make them think the government really does care about the world beyond the M25, the Integrated Regional Offices seem to have had the opposite effect. Its woken them up to what they have been missing. This is perhaps not surprising. History suggests that reform is a slippery slope. The most dangerous time for a centralised regime is when it begins to unbend.[10]

THE BRITISH DEBATE OVER ENGLISH REGIONALISM

An indication that the 'centralised regime' was beginning to 'unbend', if not crack came from John Major himself, at the end of 1994. His New Year message, in which he highlighted Labour's devolution programme in such hysterical terms — 'teenage madness' and 'one of the most dangerous propositions ever put to the British nation' had the virtue of at least foregrounding the debate. It made clear that in future the so-called integrity of the United Kingdom — the position of Scotland and Wales, but also the Regions in England — would be projected as the other side of the coin of European integration as a key battleground between Conservatives and Labour.

It also threw Labour on the defensive and forced it, for the first time in the 1990s, to do some serious thinking about its policies for the English Regions. The devil, as it is said, is in the detail. There are signs that in examining the detail Labour is making susbtantial progress compared with its position in the 1970s. The party's first instinct, however, was to backtrack, revealing the cautious, essentially conservative character of the Blair approach. Nothing — no policy, commitment or principle — should be allowed to get in the way of winning the next election. Press reports in the wake of Major's attack indicated that Blair was to scale down the commitment to powerful regional government throughout England. They would not be set up unless there was clear demand. Instead, the party would 'democratise' the Quangos and hospital trusts set up by the Tories, by bringing together an indirectly elected group of councillors for each of the English Regions. An exception would be London, which was the only capital city in Europe without an elected strategic authority.

This position was given the title 'Devolution on Demand' by the Institute for Public Policy Research (IPPR), the Left-leaning think-tank, in a paper published in May 1995. This formed the intellectual framework for the Labour policy consultation paper *A Choice for England* published the following month. The IPPR paper struck a sceptical note, suggesting that the English Regions were 'essentially artificial constructs':

> The lack of a strong regional identity in England undermines the usefulness of comparisons with our European neighbours.[11]

However, the author of the paper, Stephen Tindale, a Londoner, undermined this assertion with a strong, indeed, passionate identification with the London 'Region'.

> ... it is impossible to deny that in London there is a clear and insistent demand to be allowed our government back.

Similar attachments can be found in the South-West, certainly Cornwall, Wessex, Essex, and certainly, too, in the various Regions in the North of England, especially the North-East where there is a fully-fledged Campaign for a Northern Assembly. Regional sensibility within England is actually exceedingly strong, with a range of markers from contrasting landscapes and economies, to an astonishing range of regional accents and literary traditions.

What needs explaining is not the lack of existence of English regional identities, but why their political dimension and representation is so weak. The answer is to be found in the long record of a powerful centralised State system — bound up with the Monarchy and Parliament — starting with the Norman Conquest, a history that only now is beginning to unravel. In turn this is linked to the English tendency to think first of their position in the class structure when considering who they are, rather than their locality or community. Yet the English are as much bound up with overbearing central state structures, though in different ways, as are the Scots or the Welsh. As Raymond Williams once put it:

> It can be said that the Welsh people have been oppressed by the English for some seven centuries. Yet it can then also be said that the English people have been oppressed by the English state for even longer.[12]

Stephen Tindale reveals an underlying agenda when he unconsciously refers back to that 1976 consultation paper *Devolution: The English Dimension* and its worries about the economic integrity of the British unitary State. Tindale's version is described in a section headed 'The Social Democratic Dilemma':

> The Left's dilemma over devolution stems from the fact that its new enthusiasm for the politics of identity and locality conflicts in important respects with its historic commitment to equality. Social democracy needs to maximise the sense of community between everyone living in a state.
>
> Devolution could undermine political support for fiscal transfers, by making redistribution more visible. The Northern league in Italy supports greater regional autonomy precisely in order to preserve more of its wealth from Rome and the South. Fears about fiscal transfers were exploited by the anti-devolutionists in the 1970s. They may yet prove accurate with regard to Scotland and Wales.[13]

An answer to Tindale's 'social democratic dilemma' is actually to be found in Italy and an important study of Italian Regional government, *Making Democracy Work*, published by the American political scientist Robert Putnam in 1993. Twenty potentially powerful Regional governments were established in Italy in 1970 as part of a constitutional settlement that had been promised since the end of World War II. As institutions they were virtually identical in form, though the social, economic, political and cultural contexts in which they were implanted differed dramatically. They ranged from the pre-industrial societies of Sicily and other Regions of the South, to the post-industrial societies of Emilia Romagna, Lombardy and the others of the north. Some were Catholic and feudal; other Communist and modern.

Their experiences over the past quarter of a century have varied greatly. Some have proved relative failures — inefficient, lethargic, corrupt. But others have been remarkably successful, promoting investment and economic development, pioneering environmental standards, creating innovative, job-training centres for the young and day-care programmes for the elderly.

In his study, which traces the history of the past twenty-five years, Putnam asks the essential question: what is the explanation for these differences? He discounts government organisation, which is more or less the same from Region to Region in Italy, though of course the way government is *implemented* varies widely. Ruled out, too, are party politics and ideology, relative social stability and political harmony, population movements, and even differing levels of affluence and prosperity.

Putnam concludes that the difference is due to what he calls *social capital*, by which he means social organisations such as co-operative networks, voluntary organisations and the depth of civic society generally. The Regional democratic governments of northern Italy have on the whole worked because they were dealing with societies that valued solidarity, civic participation, and integrity. They were communities traditionally organised in a horizontal way with a highly developed degree of individual citizenship expressed through strong civic, usually voluntary, institutions.

On the other hand, Regions like Calabria and Sicily were traditionally less 'civic' in character. That is to say, they were organised more vertically, with hierarchic social structures, classically divided into peasants and bosses, in which obligations were imposed rather than mutually shared — 'Things must change so they can stay the same ...' and so on. Putnam traces the differences back more than a millennium to when republics were established in places like Florence, Bologna, and Genoa and developed traditions of civic engagement and successful government:

> For at least ten centuries, North and South have followed contrasting approaches to the dilemmas of collective action that afflict all societies. In the North norms of reciprocity and networks of civil engagement have been embodied in guilds, mutual aid societies, cooperatives, unions, and even soccer clubs and literary societies. These horizontal civic bonds have under girded levels of economic and institutional performance generally much higher than in the South, where social and political relations have been vertically structured. Although we are accustomed to thinking of the state and the market as alternative mechanisms for solving social problems this history suggests that both states and markets operate more efficiently in civic settings.[14]

THE ECONOMIC CASE RESTATED

By the same token, when Stephen Tindale poses a choice between economic regionalism and social democratic redistribution he is presenting us with a false dilemma. Redistribution and hand-outs — the old-style carrot-and-stick regional economic dispersal policies — are at best short-term responses to regional inequalities. More often than not they only serve to reinforce the underlying structural problems that persist in less-favoured regions. This is old-style regional economic thinking, more characteristic of the 1960s than the 1990s.

When it emerged Labour's consultation paper was far more incisive than Stephen Tindale's analysis. It contained a trenchant critique of the 'actually existing' regional administration and Quango state in England. It even called in aid the Right-wing thinker Karl Popper's *Poverty of Historicism* to expose its inefficiency. Popper was an ardent opponent of 'democratic centralism' — that it is always easy to centralise power, but far more difficult to centralise the information for the wise wielding of that power. Labour's document warned that the lack of a democratic regional structure meant that the English regions were losing out in Europe, quoting an Audit Commission report to this effect:

> Both the reform of the structural funds and the creation of networks are part of the EC's broader aim to expand its level of contact and policy dialogue with sub-central units of government in the community.[15]

Most importantly the Labour consultation document restates emphatically the economic case that the lack of a clear regional structure in England has made it more difficult to develop an effective regional economic policy, so pulling the emphasis away from Tindale's 'social democratic dilemma':

> England is handicapped by by a serious regional imbalance. Political, financial and economic decision-making is concentrated in the City of London and Whitehall. This has profound implications for access to investment. In order to correct this imbalance Britain needs an economic strategy which is geared to the particular needs of its regions. This can only be developed by those regions themselves.[16]

The need for regional self-motivation and self-sufficiency has to be understood in a world-wide context. It is increasingly recognised that we are witnessing a global market place in which the pace of economic and technological change is accelerating. There are now vast flows of capital at an international level and increasing inter-dependence of production activities. The globalisation of economic relations has been fostered by revolutions in communication systems and information technology.

At the same time there has been a shift towards decentralised forms of organisation and management in both the public and private sectors. Power is dispersed more widely through organisations. Structures are becoming cellular rather than pyramid-like in their formation. Global forces and multi-national companies are not impervious to spatial considerations.

There is now a growing human geography and economic literature charting the inter-connections between globalisation on the one hand, and localisation on the other.[17] Foreign direct investment by multi-national concerns is being seen as attracted to Regions which have a co-ordinated drive to innovation in specialised areas, with clusters of linked activities and firms, and supply chain networks. In this way the most dynamic of the emerging Regional economies are dovetailing naturally into the emerging global economy. The emerging global and regional economies are proving to be two sides of the same coin. The best-placed regions will be those that, through political mobilisation, have developed technology-intensive clusters of related activities. These are the 'motor' regions we hear so much about, motor regions because they are in the vanguard of learning and innovation. This is the 'bourgeois regionalism' that is explored in the next chapter. For the foreseeable future it is likely to provide the regionalist impulse with its main dynamic.

A EUROPE OF REGIONS

During the last phase of the devolution debate in Britain, in the 1970s regionalism was not perceived to be anything like as central as it is in the 1990s to economic development. Neither — from the English/British perspective at any rate — was it seen as fitting so naturally into a Europe-wide framework.

In the 1990s, however, the Regions have become a key part of the contemporary debate on the future of Europe. The nature of borders within the European Union is changing. On the one hand nation-state frontiers are breaking down, while on the other there are emerging new, sometimes much older, borders — porous certainly, but economically, culturally and politically of growing significance. The most sensitive of these new/old borders are the ones that butt against, and often actually straddle, those of the nation-states themselves. There are many examples, ranging from Catalunya, between France and Spain, to Lorraine and Saarland between France and Germany. Together they are creating new/old fault lines that are breaking up nineteenth century nation-state Europe. In the words of the Northern Ireland writer Edna Longley, these European border regions have the character of 'cultural corridors', essential communication routes in the emerging new Europe.

The new borders embrace Regions of enormous diversity — in size, history and identity. Some of the new entities are familiar — old or previously existing states like Lithuania, Serbia and Scotland, or long-standing aspirants to nationhood like Wales, Brittany or the Basque Country. Some are completely new to what hitherto we have known as western Europe, like the eastern states of Belorussia and Moldovia. Others are simply administrative units like Upper and Lower Normandy — convenient divisions of an historic region decreed from the capital of a nation-state. Still others have elements of nationality and administrative rationale, like Andalusia, Alsace, Piedmont or Wallonia. Others again were conceived bureaucratically, yet appear to be rapidly acquiring a neo-national life of their own, like the Lyons-Grenoble (Rhônes-Alpes) conurbation in France, and Baden-Wurttemberg in Germany.

It is interesting, too, that in the endless debate about what constitutes a Region, the mainstream European experience is that identity issues are paramount, rather than what might be considered more objective factors such as size or even geography. In England it seems to be assumed that a Region must have a significant population running to millions. Hence the smallest of the ten Regions defined by the new Integrated Regional Offices is the North-East, with just over three million inhabitants, while the largest is the South-East (outside London) with nearly eight million people.

In continental Europe a different tradition prevails. In Italy seven Regions (for example, Umbria) have a population of less than a million, while four (for example, Lombardy) have a population of five million. In Germany the city state of Bremen has a population of 667,000, while North Rhine Westphalia has a population of nearly seventeen million. In Spain La Rioja has a population of 263,000, while Catalunya has a population of just over six million.

However the components are defined, this mosaic is creating the idea of the 'Europe of the Regions', a structure fit for the twenty first century rather than the Nation-State Europe with its roots in the nineteenth. Accelerated European economic and political integration has resulted in the redrawing of the boundaries between market and state. The Single European Market has effectively undermined traditional nation-state regional policy and promoted the Region to a more autonomous presence, not just in the European market but in the global market as well.

Within Europe the Region has been recognised institutionally with the establishment of the Committee of the Regions. This Committee is now pressing to be given equal status with the other European Union institutions, alongside the European Parliament, the Council of Ministers, the Commission, the Court of Justice, and the Court of Auditors. A paper drawn up for presentation to the 1996 Intergovernmental Conference (IGC) on revising the Maastricht Treaty, by the President of the Committee of the Regions, Catalunya'a President Jordi Pujol, is also calling for a revision of the Treaty in the key area of subsidiarity. It wants a re-wording of the second paragraph of Article 3b of the Treaty of the Union to include specific reference to the role of the Regions:

> The Community shall take action, in accordance with the principle of subsidiarity, only if and in so far as the objectives of the proposed action cannot be sufficiently achieved by the Member States , or by the Regions and local authorities endowed with powers under the domestic legislation of the Member State in question.[18]

The Europe of the Regions remains a fluid and unfocused notion, a direction of the will rather than a blueprint. No one map can capture its sense. Yet it is on the map in the 1990s in a concrete economic way that was only dimly perceived in the 1970s, certainly so far as England is concerned. And at least one aspect of the direction now seems unmistakable: a transcendence of the rigidities of big, upper-case Nation-State nationalism by the flexibilities of small, lower-case regionalism.

NOTES

1. See the *Western Mail*, 3 July 1995, which, recording the Campaign's inaugural meeting, reports that it 'ditched its provisional title — CARP (Labour Campaign for an Assembly with Real Powers) — in order to fall into line with a Scottish campaign with similar aims, Scottish Labour Action'.
2. The interview was conducted by Philip Cooke and first published as 'Nationalisms and Popular Socialism' in *Radical Wales* 2, Spring 1984 (Cardiff Plaid Cymru). It was reprinted as 'Decentralism and the Politics of Place' in Raymond Williams *Resources of Hope* (London: Verso Books, 1989).
3. Named after the Labour MP Tam Dalyell's West Lothian constituency this draws attention to the anomaly that in a devolved Wales and Scotland, Welsh and Scottish MPs at Westminster would continue to to able to vote on English matters concerning education, the health service and so on, whereas English MPs would not be able to vote on the same matters as they apply to Wales and Scotland. Yet, as the peoples of Wales and Scotland know only too well, MPs at Westminster are con-

tinually voting on matters that do not affect their own constituents' interests. In any event it would be surprising if a convention did not emerge that, whenever specifically English concerns were debated and voted upon, Welsh and Scottish MPs would refrain from participating. This would allow England to pursue divergent policies in such fields as education and the health service. Therein lies the problem for Labour centralists. However, to state the problem only demonstrates the reality that over-rigid symmetry in constitutional structures can be a negation rather than enhancement of genuine democracy.

4. *Devolution: The English Dimension* - A Consultative Document, HMSO, December 1976.

5. Labour Regional Policy Working Group *Alternative Regional Strategy: A Framework for Discussion*, September 1982.

6.Business in the Community and Coopers & Lybrand *Lessons from continental Europe: Promoting partnership for local economic development and business support in the UK* (Business in the Community, 227a City Road, London EC1V 1LX, 1992).

7. David Hunt, then Secretary of State for Employment, speech to the Institute of Directors, February 1994.

8. *The Independent on Sunday*, 5 February 1995.

9. Hansard, Vol 252, Col 275, 16 January 1995.

10. Howard Davies, speech to regional newspaper editors, London, 6.February 1995.

11. Stephen Tindale *Devolution on Demand — options for the English regions and London* (IPPR, 30-32 Southampton Road, London WC2E 7RA, May 1995).

12. Raymond Williams, 'Wales and England' in John Osmond (ed.) *The National Question Again - Welsh Political Identity in the 1980s* (Llandysul: Gomer Press, 1985), p.18.

13. Stephen Tindale *op.cit.* p.9-10.

14. Robert D. Putnam, *Making Democracy Work — Civic Traditions in Modern Italy* (Princeton University Press, 1993), p.181.

15. Audit Commission Report *A Rough Guide to Europe*, HMSO, December 1991, p. 40.

16. *A choice for England* - A consultation paper on Labour's plans for English regional government (Labour Party, John Smith House, 150 Walworth Road, London SE17 1JT, July 1995).

17. See, for instance the paper produced by Michael Storper of the Lewis Center for Regional Policy Studies, University of California, in September 1991: *Technology Districts and International Trade - The Limits to Globalization in an Age of Flexible production*

18. European Union Committee of the Regions, *Opinion on the Revision of the Treaty on European Union* (Brussels, 20 April 1995).

WELSH EUROPEANS

Since the early 1960s Welsh consciousness has been undergoing a subtle but fundamental transformation. The process has entailed a gradual but nonetheless profound resolution of a contradiction at the core of Welsh politics — an identity conflict between Britishness on the one hand and Welshness on the other. The resolution is far from complete. Most Welsh people, when they stop to think about it, probably still cling to a duality of feeling between a sense of both Wales and Britain, the attachments varying according to time and occasion. Unlike the English, Britishness has a specificity of its own for the Welsh. In part this can be traced to ancient Welsh mythologies around 'The Island of Britain', a matter to which we will need to return. For the most part, however, it is connected with British state institutions, such as the Crown, Parliament and the armed forces. Lacking distinctive institutions of their own, and relying for the most part on cultural markers to sustain their sense of themselves as a distinct people, the Welsh have clung to the institutions of their neighbours.

Yet since the 1950s history has been driving Welsh people away from Britishness and towards a new duality in which belonging to Wales is felt more and more in conjunction with a sense of belonging to Europe. We are becoming Welsh Europeans.

The decade when this movement became clearly visible was the 1960s when a number of key institutions were established and Welsh nationalism made its political breakthrough. The Welsh Office and BBC Wales were founded (both, coincidentally, in 1964); Conservative followed by Labour administrations began negotiations to enter what was then the European Common Market; Cymdeithas yr Iaith Gymraeg began its vivid campaign for the language; and in 1966 Plaid Cymru won Carmarthen by-election, thereby forcing the Welsh Labour and trade union movement to begin a long and often painful re-positioning of itself in relation to Wales. The Wales TUC was founded in 1973 in what at the time was a unilateral declaration of independence from the British (England and Wales) TUC.

Raymond Williams charted the shift, most clearly in the history of his own attitudes and feelings towards Wales during the period. He it was who first described himself as a 'Welsh

European', in 1978, a time when for most Welsh people the idea would have seemed both distant and exotic. Within a decade, however, the 'structure of feeling' engaged in this formulation had entered the mainstream consciousness of the Welsh intellectual left. Raymond Williams described the process in a key passage in Politics and Letters , the volume of interviews conducted with him by the editors of *New Left Review*. Asked to relate the history of his relationship with Wales he recalled that the key change had started to happen from the late 1960s:

> There was a continuity in a quite overwhelming feeling about the land of Wales; as feeling and writing that stays through. But then I began having many more contacts with Welsh writers and intellectuals, all highly political in the best tradition of the culture, and I found this curious effect. Suddenly England, bourgeois England, wasn't my point of reference any more. I was a Welsh European, and both levels felt different. There's still a lot to work through from that, but I can hardly describe the difference of talking and relating now in Wales, with writers and political comrades who are all hard up against it — what's seen from outside is a remarkable vitality, and so it objectively is, but there it's a hard, fierce, internally contending yet bitterly communal feeling, which is also where I happen to be and now in the truest sense to be from.
>
> Through the intricacies of the politics, and they are very intricate indeed, I want the Welsh people — still a radical and cultured people — to defeat, override or bypass bourgeois England; the alternatives follow from the intricacies. That connects for me with the sense in my work that I am now necessarily European; that the people to the left and on the left of the French and Italian communist parties, the German and Scandinavian comrades, the communist dissidents from the East like Bahro, are my kind of people; the people I come from and belong to, and my more conscious Welshness is, as I feel it, my way of learning those connections. I mean that over a whole range, from when Welsh-speaking nationalists tell me, as if I needed to be reassured, how thoroughly Welsh *Border Country* and the social thinking are — which I used not to realise — to when highly cosmopolitan Welsh intellectuals offer recognition of the whole range of my work, which literally none of my English official colleagues has seen a chance of making sense of, then I am in a culture where I can breathe ...[1]

'THE ISLAND OF BRITAIN'

This statement was published in 1979, the year of the referendum in which the Welsh, on the face of it, voted themselves out of existence. Certainly, one interpretation of the 1979 referendum and its four-to-one rejection of a democratic Assembly, was that the inhabitants of Wales had chosen the British dimension of their identity which seemed to require the elimination of the Welsh one.

At the same time, in 1979, others declared that Britain, certainly the British State, was entering a long period of dissolution, gradually exchanging an imperial identity for a European one. In a famous lecture the historian Gwyn A. Williams remarked on the irony that at just this juncture — in the European and General Elections of 1979 as well as the referendum — the Welsh registered their country as the most passionately and emphatically British of all the various regions and nations of the United Kingdom. 'We Welsh look like being the last of the British,' he declared. 'There is some logic in this. We were, after all, the First'.[2]

As stated earlier, ideas of Britain, specifically of the 'Island of Britain' — which in another curious paradox rarely extend beyond Hadrian's Wall — go deep into Welsh memory and mythology. The ascension of Henry VII to the English throne after the Battle of Bosworth in 1485, at the head of a largely Welsh-speaking army, was felt by many at the time to be a fulfilment of the Arthurian myth that he would return. In acknowledgement Henry named his first-born son Arthur.

It was the London Welshman Dr John Dee who in the time of Elizabeth I invented the idea and coined the name of the British Empire.[3] In the industrial revolution it was south Wales that became a human melting pot for the British identity, producing the coal that fuelled the British fleet. Lloyd George was felt to be another Arthurian incarnation, regaining once more the island of Britain for the Welsh. Such a sensibility has never been part of Scottish historical mythology and goes a long way to describe the difference between the two countries.

Dafydd Glyn Jones has made the same point by drawing attention to the advice offered to the Welsh on their relations with the English by the little known writer, William Williams of Llandygai, in his book *Prydnawngwaith y Cymry* (The Noonday of the Welsh People), published in 1822:

> From what has already been related we observe that we the Welsh, the sole remnant of the ancient Britons, are incorporated and made one with the English, the race of our fathers' erstwhile enemies; and God be praised — we have the same rights and privileges as themselves, so that the most arrogant among them cannot inflict upon us the least injustice; we have the same law as themselves to defend us; therefore we have aught to do but to chew our food, and hold our tongues, and above all avoid being contentious.[4]

As Dafydd Glyn Jones observes, this is entirely representative of the old — and still enduring — Welsh patriotic tradition, its accommodation with Britishness and the politics of demobilisation: 'It is British, it is anti-English. Vainglory and guilt, pride and subservience are all mixed up within it'. Yet the contradiction inherent in this adherence to Britishness — exemplified by those, especially on the left, who urged the No vote in the 1979 referendum — is that, to be sustainable, it demands that the peoples of the rest of the island share in the same identity. Plainly they do not. The English may sometimes call themselves British, and like Churchill believe they are an 'island race'. In truth, however, they are simply and straight forwardly English.

As Dafydd Glyn Jones also remarks, David Jones was perhaps the one serious cultural figure who could say, 'In me, Britain is one' and mean it. He was half Welsh, half Londoner who spent most of his life in London. As an infantryman on the Western Front he found himself a member of a mixed regiment of Londoners and Welshmen. No two groups, he commented, could have been more different, yet in their coming together they were representative. 'Together they bore in their bodies the genuine tradition of the Island of Britain,' he declared.

David Jones' vision was unique. As Dafydd Glyn Jones says, that was the only thing wrong with it. A problem for the Welsh is that there is no such thing as a British nationality in which all the people of Britain can participate and which is distinguishable from English nationality.

TORY BRITAIN

What 'British nation' did John Major have in mind when he warned in a BBC Radio 4 interview at the New Year in 1994-5 that Labour's plans for Scotland and Wales constituted 'one of the most dangerous propositions' that have ever been put before it? Was it the same one that he ruminated upon during the Maastricht debates, that ever enduring land of village greens, warm beer and spinsters riding to church on their bicycles ?

A year earlier Michael Portillo issued another warning about 'one of the greatest threats that has ever confronted the British nation'. This time it was the press and media that were doing their best to undermine the country's national pride and institutions. The relations that hold society together, Portillo said, stretch from

> ...the top to the bottom. If Crown, Parliament and Church are not respected, neither will be the law, judges, policemen, nor professors, nor social workers, nor bosses, managers or foremen. Social disorder follows when respect breaks down.[5]

What is clear, then, is that if the British nation exists other than in the imagination of anxious Conservative leaders, it resides in the great institutions of State — Monarchy and Parliament — which stretch from 'the top to the bottom'. At the bottom are Us the people, subjects (under the Crown) straining to become citizens. The danger to the 'British nation' is that the people are becoming restive and thinking about transforming Britain from the bottom up. This is the real significance of Labour's devolution plans, not just for Wales and Scotland but, as we have seen in the previous chapter, for the Regions of England as well.

The impact is likely to be most keenly felt in England. As John Major correctly but only dimly perceives, England will have to re-negotiate how it imagines itself in relation to Britain. What does being British mean for the English? The Welsh and Scots are at least used to the question. For the English, however, the matter is altogether more perplexing, not to say irritating. As Michael Portillo went on to say to the Conservative Way Forward group in January 1994, 'Britain has been unusually fortunate in that as an island nation we have for centuries rarely had to think about how we define ourselves.'

It is undoubtedly the case, as we have seen, that the Scots, and certainly the Welsh, are far more self-consciously British than the English. There have even been times — during the high points of Empire and the wars of this century for instance —when they have for all intents and purposes merged their identities into a British national consciousness. This, however, could never be possible for the English who have long adopted a quite different, if seldom articulated, relationship with Britain. For them this is felt as an idea of Greater England, a kind of fusion of England — as defined by its borders with Wales and Scotland — with the island as a whole. The resultant identity can best be described as Anglo-British.

The process has been a consequence of a complex interaction of the geography and historical development of the British Isles with the institutions that have evolved, especially the monarchy and Parliament, and the relationship of the whole with the wider world. As is now becoming a mainstream historical view, the critical period for the fusion of England with Britain began with the Civil War of the mid-seventeenth century and the accommodation between monarchy and Parliament of 1688. At that moment a popular, democratic and republican idea of England and Englishness was smothered, so to speak, at birth.

Instead, what developed as events unfolded, was a curious identity, reliant more on institutions than people and more on territory abroad than at home. It was an identity forged and tested through the period of the Napoleonic Wars when democratic and republican, revolutionary, and above all Catholic, France was faced down by monarchical and oligarchic, Protestant, Greater England. This was the heroic period of the Anglo-British whose twin gladiators, Wellington and Nelson, still dominate the high ramparts of the nation's capital.[6]

The victory, from 1793 to 1815, was the foundation for the industrial revolution and imperial expansion of the last century and the identity constructed, and then sustained by the monarchy more than any other institution, was further maintained until the 1950s by two more European civil wars. Since then, however, Anglo-Britishness and the idea of the British nation has lapsed into a kind of nostalgic nationalism, kept alive in a permanent respiratory chamber by the annual round of royal and Parliamentary occasions and commemorative ceremonies such as Remembrance Day. Rarely, and only when freak circumstances combine, the inert figure jerks into life. Such was the occasion of the Falklands Campaign when, once more 'an island race', 'standing alone' and surrounded by 'a cruel sea' confronted a foreign dictator.[7]

It was a perfect, and very lucky, opportunity for Mrs Thatcher to discover her project of putting the 'Great' back into Britain. Another revealing instance was her instruction in 1984 that the underground Cabinet War rooms in Whitehall, used by Churchill during the early years of World War II, should be opened to the public. Over the next few years they were visited by more than a million people.

In *The English World* a lavishly illustrated account of the identity being discussed here, Robert Blake begins his introduction with the reflection that the country's coastline has helped to shape both the history of the English nation and the psychology of the English character. A paragraph later he adds, 'We come back to the cliché that Britain is an island, a fact that has been subtly decisive in so many aspects of her history: in the Reformation, which determined the course of religion in England ...' On and on this litany goes, but note the elision of Britain into England in the same sentence.[8]

The core of this identity is geographically very small: built around Oxbridge and central London and its outer ring — the significantly-named Home Counties — and linked to institutions like the armed forces, the Monarchy and Parliament. 'Britain abroad' — the far-flung Empire/Commonwealth —is less easy to include these days (even less our American 'cousins' except perhaps within the espionage genre) but it still resonates, as the Falklands episode demonstrated. The roots of this identity point upwards into class-based hierarchies, rather than downwards into lived communities. Even so it is idle to ignore their strength nor the passion of those who cling to them.

When John Major speaks of threats to this Anglo-British identity, to the 'Union', he does so with a sudden, almost choking, discovery of emotion. What is the source of this British nationalism and pride? More revealingly, from whom is it coming? More often than not the politicians who articulate it are in some way marginal to English identity in an unambiguously English sense. Examine some of the 'British' nationalist politicians: Teddy Taylor, a Scot evicted by the electorate from his Glasgow seat and adopted by Southend; John Redwood, a lower middle class recruit from Dover sent, via All Souls, the City and Downing Street to rule Wales; Michael Howard and Malcolm Rifkind, both of Jewish Lithuanian stock, ascending the greasy pole in Disraeli's image from base camps in Llanelli and Edinburgh; Michael Portillo, whose forbears hail from Spain and supported the Republican side in the Spanish Civil War. Even John Major himself, though plainly a Londoner in origin, had a skewed lower-middle class trajectory into the upper echelons of the Tory high command, avoiding the usual paths through public school and Oxbridge or, indeed, any university. All these positions of inherent insecurity suggestive of a need to accentuate rather than effortlessly assume an identity.

THE NEW EUROPE

The 'Europe of the Regions', explored in the previous chapter, is the context within which a Welsh alternative to Britishness is being worked through. This is the process through which we are becoming Welsh Europeans. The project has been around in various forms for some time, and certainly since the early decades of this century. It was Saunders Lewis, for example, who declared, in 1927, that :

> To bring political and economic unity to Europe should be one of the first priorities of our century.

In this enterprise Wales was to play a grand role. A condition for the success of a European union was that the countries of Britain be part of it. And of these Wales was the only one with an unambiguous European tradition:

> The Welsh are the only nation in Britain who have been part of the Roman Empire, who in childhood, were weaned on the milk of the West, and who have the blood of the West in their veins.[9]

If this sounds apocalyptic it was meant to. 'Wales can understand Europe, for she is one of the family,' Saunders Lewis continued. Nonetheless, the assertion bears further examination. In his *Principles of Nationalism* (1926) Saunders Lewis outlined his vision for a modern Welsh nation by expressing it as freedom rather than independence within a united Europe. This Europe would be one that returned to medieval times when the Pope ruled supreme, but allowing diversity for nations within the unity of a single Christian authority. The deracinated Welshman, Henry VII, followed by his surviving son Henry VIII, had muddied the waters by opposing the Pope and setting in train modern nation-statism. This was a trajectory that led, he said, more or less directly to World War I. Nationalism as practised in this history was to be eschewed. Instead, we were to look forward to a more civilised and benign small-nation nationalism (spelt, perhaps, with a small 'n') in which Wales once more could play a meaningful if not leading part.

Expressed in terms of the 1990s, for the Pope read the European Commission, and for the idea of unity and diversity, read the patchwork quilt of 'L'Europe aux Cents Drapeaux' or 'The Europe of the Regions'. In two books that appeared in the early 1990s, *Cultural Weapons* and *The Rise of Regional Europe*, Christopher Harvie, an historian who has connections with both Scotland and Wales, subjected this notion — perhaps by now it warrants the status of a world-view or *Weltanschauung* — to some serious analysis in terms of what is actually happening on the ground. In doing so he performed a useful service in obliging us to confront some uncomfortable, not to say unpalatable realities. A primary insight is that Welsh nationalism's preoccupation, following on from Saunders Lewis, with linguistic minorities within Europe, with other parts of the Celtic forest so to speak, has been less than helpful in revealing the actual dynamics of the emerging Europe of the Regions. Instead, says Harvie, we should be focusing on the core regions, the Four Motors (Baden-Wurttemberg, Rhônes-Alpes, Lombardy and Catalunya) and what he describes as 'bourgeois regionalism'.

In this endeavour the first difficulty is a lack of clarity about terms. What, after all is a 'Region' and where does the idea described by a 'Europe of the Regions' begin and end? For instance, for the purposes of what we now have to refer to as the European Union (rather than Community), a Europe of the Regions might include the Czech Republic but not, perhaps, Slovakia. In one sense, too, Christopher Harvie would want Scotland to be thought of as a Region. Yet towards the end of *Cultural Weapons*, which has the subtitle 'Scotland and Survival in a New Europe', he remarks:

> Its because there are other things more important than the material well-being of the Scottish people that the maximum of self-government is essential. We have in Mazzini's terms, a duty rather than a right to take part in world politics as a nation, not just to hang around the corridors of Brussels as just another region, cap in hand...[10]

The main point, however, is that, from the Welsh nationalist perspective, up to somewhere in the mid-1980s, European Regions began with Wales, Scotland, Brittany, Corsica, Euskadi, Galicia, Sardinia and other peripheral, what might be described as 'culture-nations' struggling to preserve languages and the economic consequences of uneven development. By and large they fitted into Michael Hechter's internal colonialism thesis, as described in his influential but diversionary book of the same name.[11]

Then, from somewhere in the early to mid-1980s European Regions gained a capital 'R' and began to achieve political credibility. The German Regions, the Lander, had been in place since the end of World War II, put their ironically by the British and the Americans as a protection against the German tendency to centralisation. Until the mid-1980s, however, the significance of the German federal system for the future structure of the European Community was scarcely appreciated. Moreover, in the mid-1980s effective devolution in Italy was little more than a decade old and the new Spanish Constitution, replacing Franco's regime with seventeen Autonomous Communities, had only just been ratified. In France, too, Mitterand's far-reaching creation of twenty-two democratically elected Regions had only just begun, in a very small way in 1982.

Since then, in what historically must be seen as an astonishingly rapid evolution, Regional Europe has emerged into view, still much less powerful than Nation-State Europe to be sure, but visible nonetheless. Not only that, it has a panoply of pan-European institutions to support it — the Assembly of European Regions, the Committee of the Regions and more than eighty Regional embassies in Brussels (including ones for Wales, Scotland, Northern Ireland, and some English regional groupings, including Essex which, for this purpose declares itself to be a Region) — and a vision of a new Europe modelled on the German federal structure.

The further important point to note is that this evolution has, for the most part, been built upon Christopher Harvie's bourgeois regions rather than on the culture nations of our former imagination. For the most part since we should not forget the most evolved 'Regions' of them all, Flanders and Wallonia in fast disappearing Belgium, and also Catalunya and Euskadi in Spain. Even so, for this argument the core remains France and Germany, and here bourgeois regionalism reigns supreme. As Harvie perceptively notes, all the four Motor Regions have the following elements in common: 'a high quality of urban life plus an absence of the headquarters of major government or international bodies, such as is to be found in London, Brussels, Paris or Geneva'.[12] So they set about creating their own institutions and also their own international links, most importantly the high-technology cartel in the shape of the Four Motors organisation to which Wales has attached itself.

Of course, reference to the relatively rich Four Motor regions emphasises the point that, as Harvie puts it, 'some regions are more equal than others'. In other words, they can be seen as an association of the haves ranged against the have-nots. This is the view of those, especially on the English/British Left, who insist that the notion of 'A Europe of the Regions' is a romantic fantasy, fuelled as Martin Kettle, the *Guardian* columnist put it, by those 'generalising from the Scottish particular and indulging in wishful escapism from the British nation state'.[13]

Christopher Harvie acknowledges part of this argument when he observes that in the 1980s Baden-Wurttemberg was the chief destination for incoming investment from the United Kingdom, itself the largest single investor in the Federal Republic in that period. Its growth was thus at the expense of UK regional development. Elsewhere, in *Cultural Weapons,* he amplifies the point:

> 'Bourgeois regionalist' movements in Europe have about them a strong sense of exclusivity among the already privileged. Perhaps the most effective of them has been the Conservative distortion of the government of Britain into promotion of South-East England, Nimbya, the land of Essex man. The politicisation of other under-privileged regions — Corsica, Ulster, Euskadi — has become locked in communal tension and violence.[14]

Yet political and economic development is invariably steered by the strongest elements in any system. The main question raised is not blindly to deny the system as such but, as ever, how best to organise redistribution of the accumulated surplus. Martin Kettle, for instance, in the same article quoted above goes on to accuse the German Lander of threatening to make not just Germany, but Europe ungovernable by 'increasing inter-regional debt problems'. Yet the whole story is much more complicated. German federalism is the sheet anchor of the Federal Republic's democracy, and the Lander governments insistence on partnership between government and industry at the regional level has been the secret of its prosperity. The 'Europe of the Regions' programme, for that is what it is becoming, aims to extend these messages to the whole of the European Union.

In this project Chris Harvie, unconsciously echoing Saunders Lewis, reserves a special role for the countries of Britain. He argues persuasively, that though Britain's regions are as yet nowhere near as developed politically as those on continental Europe, generally speaking they have a greater cultural depth, a greater sense of identity and coherence based on cultural as well as economic markers. This, he says, applies not only to Wales and Scotland, but to the English regions as well. Harvie concludes *The Rise of Regional Europe* with the thought that :

> The natural regionality of the British Isles — the persistence of distinct national traditions and the comparative strength of civil society — could be of enormous value to a federated Europe, while the assertion of a 'British' identity by Conservative politicians such as Lady Thatcher and Lord Tebbit smacks more of a lack of confidence in the British state.[15]

That might be considered over-optimistic, especially when faced with the persistent lack of political expression by the English regions. Yet as we have seen in the previous chapter, even the Conservative government established the administrative framework for English regionalism — the ten Integrated Regional Offices — and the Labour Party is developing a rolling programme for democratic devolution to take them over. These developments came too late to be embraced by Christopher Harvie in *The Rise of Regional Europe*, but it surely bears out his case. Moreover, it illuminates what would previously have been more easily considered a fanciful aside in the earlier volume, *Cultural Weapons*:

> ... the coincidence of British economic collapse with the achievement of the European project suggests that Britain might 'implode' into the European Community. This would be no bad thing: a Britain which perceived all its possibilities in European politics might give European institutions a flexibility and effectiveness, presently lacking, which could accelerate the integration of other powers, especially Germany ... 'These islands', as the Irish put it, could become a useful prototype for the environmentally-based supra-regional grouping which must evolve within the new Europe.[16]

To put it another way, as Welsh Europeans we have a twenty first century role. This could be in the ambitious sense envisaged here or, as seems more likely, in some rather more traditional form in which the nation-states continue to have a powerful presence. They would continue in a 'leading' postion, but nonetheless one in which they were obliged to collaborate in ever more formal relationships with pan-European structures above, and Regional and local structures below.

A final word on this should be allowed Raymond Williams whose vision, from the mid-1970s, this clearly was. He made it plain in one of the last interviews he gave, in 1987:

> Coming from a border area of Wales ... the problem for me has always been one of what it was to be Welsh — I mean in some serious sense, rather than in one of the exportable stage-Welsh versions. I suppose there was some group I thought of as the *real* Welsh, secure in their identity, who would come out in force and flail this returning immigrant with all his doubts.
>
> The response I've had, especially from young Welsh people, has been precisely the opposite: thank God someone has come out and asked who are we, what are we? All my usual famous qualifying and complicating, my insistence on depths and ambiguities, was exactly what they already knew. And this experience of ambiguity and contradiction hasn't only equipped us in Wales to understand our situation better; it's also equipped us, emotionally and intellectually, to understand the situation of increasing numbers of people —

> including the once so self-assured, confident English. Its easier for us, in other words, to put questions to those simple, confident, unitary identities which really belong to an earlier historical period.[17]

There is, of course, a continuing duality of identity here, as Williams says, just as there was in the previous division between Welshness and Britishness. But now, instead of a debilitating split there is the potential for a creative integration. In unifying Wales with Europe there is the prospect of a resolution rather than a clash of contradiction. This evolution of identity is equipping Wales for effective participation in the twenty-first century. The trajectory is typical of Williams' own life project: the seeking of an integrating wholeness. Being Welsh and also European can, indeed, be a resource of hope as the next century approaches. In-between there is, as Williams also says, a culture in which we can breathe.

NOTES

1. Raymond Williams, *Politics and Letters* (London: New Left Books, 1979), pp.295-6.
2. Gwyn A. Williams, *When Was Wales?*, the BBC Cymru/Wales 1979 annual radio lecture; reprinted in *The Welsh* in their history (London: Croom Helm, 1982).
3. Gwyn A. Williams, *Welsh Wizard and British Empire: Dr John Dee and a Welsh Identity*, third annual Gwyn Jones Lecture at University College, Cardiff, 1982; reprinted in *The Welsh in Their History* (London: Croom Helm, 1982).
4. Quoted by Dafydd Glyn Jones in *The Secret of the Island of Britain*, BBC Cymru/Wales annual radio lecture, 1992, p. 10.
5. Michael Portillo, speech to the Conservative Way Forward President's annual dinner, 14 January 1994. A long edited extract from the speech was carried by *The Independent on Sunday*, 16 January 1994, under the heading 'Poison of a new British disease'.
6. This history has been brilliantly traced by Linda Colley in her book *Britons — Forging the Nation 1707-1837* (Yale University Press,1992).
7. See Anthony Barnett's *Iron Britannia - Why Parliament waged its Falklands War* (London: Allison and Busby, 1982).
8. Robert Blake (ed.) *The English World* (London: Thames and Hudson, 1982). The quotation is taken from his introduction 'The Englishness of England', p.8.
9. *Y Ddraig Goch*, Plaid Cymru, November 1927. See Dafydd Glyn

Jones's essay on 'His Politics', in Alun R. Jones and Gwyn Thomas (eds.) *Presenting Saunders Lewis* (Cardiff: University of Wales Press, 1973), pp.32-3.

10. Christopher Harvie, *Cultural Weapons — Scotland and Surivival in a New Europe* (Edinburgh: Polygon, 1992), p.109.

11. Michael Hechter, *Internal Colonialism - The Celtic Fringe in British National Development, 1536-1966* (London: Routledge & Kegan Paul, 1975).

12. Christopher Harvie, *The Rise of Regional Europe* (London: Routledge, 1993), p.66.

13. *The Guardian*, 25 April 1992.

14. Christopher Harvie, *Cultural Weapons, op. cit.*, p.34.

15. Christopher Harvie, *The Rise of Regional Europe, op.cit.*, p.74.

16. *Cultural Weapons, op.cit.*, p. 34.

17. Raymond Williams, *Resources of Hope*, Verso 1989, p. 320.

MOVEMENTS FOR A DEMOCRATIC WALES

In the mid-1990s, as the movement gathers pace for finally achieving a democratic Wales, it is worth glancing back at some key moments in our rcent history. We've been around a similar track arguing the case for a Welsh Parliament on more than one occasion in the past fifty years — an experience that bears testimony to the old adage that those who fail to learn their own history are condemned to relive it. Some of these past episodes throw a good deal of light on our present circumstances. Many of the pressures that afflict the current determination of policy and, indeed, the terms of much of the debate itself, have not changed a great deal. Where opposition has been overcome in the past, it can be overcome again.

In July 1950, for instance, the Parliament for Wales Campaign of that era was launched at a conference in Llandrindod. It was attended by a wide cross-section of Welsh political figures including Lady Megan Lloyd George (then Liberal MP for Anglesey) Sir Ifan ab Owen Edwards, and a number of leading Labour councillors, trade unionists and the Labour MP for Merthyr, S.O. Davies, who declared:

> Control of their own affairs must be handed to Wales and Scotland. We either do that, or we lose the measure of freedom that parliamentary democracy guarantees us.[1]

The Welsh Regional Council of Labour was not best pleased. They organised their own rally on the same day, in Newtown. And their secretary, Cliff Prothero, wrote stern letters to the National Executive in London and the Merthyr Trades Council complaining about S.O. Davies' presence at the Llandrindod conference which, he said, had been 'convened as a result of agitation by the Welsh Nationalists'.[2]

In March 1994 another conference was held at Llandrindod, to promote the same aims as those in 1950, by the present-day Parliament for Wales Campaign. Again on the same day the

Wales Labour Party organised their own conference, this time at Newport, to launch their European election campaign. The four MPs who attended the Llandrindod event — Peter Hain (Neath), Jon Owen Jones (Cardiff Central), John Marek (Wrexham) and Paul Flynn (Newport West) were called to account in acrimonious terms by the Welsh Labour Executive. In 1950 when S.O. Davies was similarly called to account he responded vigorously. He told the Merthyr Trades Council that it was the the Welsh Regional Council of Labour rather than himself who were 'not in line with the movement in Wales'.[3] There are signs in the 1990s that on this score, history is repeating itself once more.

BEVAN VERSUS GRIFFITHS

The main achievement of the Parliament for Wales Campaign of the 1950s was to be part of the pressure that put the creation of a Secretary of State for Wales on the political agenda. By the end of the decade the Labour Party was seriously contemplating it. In the 1950s establishing a Welsh Office was the nearest equivalent to creating a Parliament or Assembly in the 1990s, and it engendered a debate whose echoes can be clearly heard in our own era. The main protagonists were Jim Griffiths and Aneurin Bevan, with Bevan vigorously opposing the idea until suddenly, in 1959, he reversed his position in a decisive intervention that placed us on the path we find ourselves following today. The source of Aneurin Bevan's initial hostility was analysed by Griffiths himself, in his memoirs:

> Nye's doubts about the creation of a Welsh Office went beyond considerations of administration. He has related how he came to realise that if he was to achieve his objectives, and his burning desire to create a Socialist society, it was imperative to reach out from the valley, and beyond the county, to the centre, where the levers of power were operated. He was impatient with nationalism which divided peoples and enslaved nations within their narrow geographical and spiritual frontiers. He feared that devolution of authority would divorce Welsh political activity from the mainstream of British politics, as he felt was already happening in Scotland.[4]

Why Bevan should have changed his line long puzzled historians. The best account has come from T.W. Jones, MP for Meirionnydd in the 1950s, who was a member of the Labour Home Policy Committee at the time. Later he revealed how in successive meetings Bevan and Griffiths argued the case until Hugh Gaitskell, the Labour leader in the chair, pronounced that they could not go on for ever and must come to a resolution at the next meeting. T.W. Jones recalled that afterwards he followed Bevan and Griffiths into the House of Commons corridor, still arguing, until they stopped. Bevan turned to Griffiths and said words to the effect:

> You really want this thing, don't you ?
> Griffiths replied:
> With all my heart and soul.[5]

This suggests that Griffiths convinced Bevan by the emotional commitment of his own approach, if not with an emotional spasm. But the papers of T.W. Jones's brother, J. Idwal Jones, MP for Wrexham during the 1950s, have thrown some further light on the matter, and suggest that Bevan had a keen intellectual appreciation of the case as well.[6] The papers record a further meeting in the Commons, of the Labour Tripartite Committee, which discussed devolution in July 1959 and lasted two hours. Present were Jim Griffiths, this time in the chair, Gaitskell, Bevan, several Welsh MPs, and representatives of the Welsh Council of Labour, including Cliff Prothero.

Gaitskell gave a résumé of the possible options. These were (i) a Royal Commission on Devolution; (ii) a Welsh Grand Committee; or (iii) a Minister for Welsh Affairs with a seat in the Cabinet. Gaitskell himself stated that if the third option were adopted he felt that such a Minister 'should have something to do'.

Bevan then spoke. Idwal Jones records that 'as usual he was brilliant, humorous, and his ideas at times scintillating'. He disposed of the idea of a Royal Commission and a Grand Committee, dismissing the latter 'as an exercise in shadow boxing'. He then demolished the proposal for a Minister in the Cabinet with no departmental responsibilities in the following terms:

> What is the use of this proposal. What is he to do? Is he

> to sit down, listening to other people talk, travel from place to place, with nothing to do but a title to carry? Is that what you want?

Ness Edwards (MP for Caerphilly) and Cliff Prothero were dumbfounded by Bevan's new approach. Edwards persistently interrupted subsequent speakers. He linked the proposal for a Secretary of State with the Welsh Nationalists and the Parliament for Wales Campaign but his arguments seemed unconvincing. Idwal Jones then described what followed:

> ... Aneurin walked up to Gaitskell, and whispered something in his ear.
> He returned and resumed his seat.
> Then he turned to me and addressed me personally.
> 'Now Idwal,' he proceeded, 'if we set up a Minister for Welsh Affairs — or call him what you like — with Cabinet rank and with department responsibility for Education, Health, Housing and Local Government, will you be satisfied?
> 'Most certainly: that is all I want.'
> 'And you Tudor?'
> 'Yes, of course,' said Tudor Watkins (MP for Brecon and Radnor).
> Then Ness (Edwards) tried again to intervene, by referring to 'perpetuating a conflict'. Aneurin had had enough.
> 'What do you mean by perpetuating a conflict,' he said. 'What conflict can there be in an advance? The Minister is there: the Office is there: and you have agreed to give him Cabinet rank. What is the conflict when you decide on giving him something definite to do?'
> 'And make him subject to other Ministers,' interrupted Ness.
> 'No, No, No,' retorted Bevan. 'Responsible to the Cabinet.'

These arguments over whether the Office of Secretary of State for Wales should be granted effective executive power and authority foreshadowed the contemporary debates over what constitutes effective power and authority for an Assembly or Parliament, discussed in Chapter 1. Is secondary legislation enough, or is primary legislative authority necessary? Should an Assembly have discretion over its own finances, or be dependent entirely on a block grant from Whitehall?

When in 1958 Harold Macmillan, the Prime Minister, rejected out of hand a detailed memorandum from the Council of Wales and Monmouthshire, pressing the case for a Secretary of State, the Council resigned en bloc. The chairman of the Council, the Transport and General Workers union leader Huw T. Edwards, declared in a famous statement:

> Whitehallism has not the slightest prospect of ever understanding Welsh aspirations.[7]

Whatever emerges as Labour's policy on an Assembly, we can expect a rearguard action at Westminster when the legislation comes to be put into effect. Certainly, this was the case in 1964 when the incoming Labour government set up the Welsh Office. It was extracted out of the Ministry of Housing and Local Government whose new Minister, Richard Crossman, recorded in his diary:

> Another equally idiotic creation is the Department for Wales, a completely artificial new office for Jim Griffiths and his two Parliamentary secretaries, all the result of a silly election pledge.[8]

A group of Welsh MPs, led by Ness Edwards, sent a memo to Harold Wilson, urging that Jim Griffiths' powers be confined to having oversight of other department functions, rather than having transferred administrative functions of his own. Jim Griffiths threatened resignation if this were to prove the case.[9] In the event he took over control of housing, local government and roads. It was to be another five years before health and education were transferred and only in the 1970s were significant economic powers gained by the Welsh Office. As can be seen from the contemporary debates, described in the opening chapter, thirty years on from the 1960s the arguments inside the Welsh Labour movement that characterised the advance to the Welsh Office have not changed fundamentally.

UDI BY THE TUC

The recognition of a distinctive Welsh economy as an integral part of Welsh politics is central to the politics of devolution. In

1973 the main impetus in this recognition was provided by the creation of the Wales TUC which came about as a result of an 'unilateral declaration of independence' (UDI) from the TUC in London. The initiative reflected the changes that had occurred in Wales during the 1960s. They included the creation of the Welsh Office, the advance of Plaid Cymru, and the resulting debates inside the Welsh Labour Party — all of which produced a growing sensitivity to Welsh demands. In institutional terms the creation of the Wales TUC, and the manner in which it was set up, was the most important development on the Welsh political scene since the establishment of the Welsh Office in 1964.

A twenty-year debate preceded the decision finally to set up the Wales TUC. The nature of the debate closely followed that over devolution itself. So much so, in fact, that it was possible to argue that once the question of the Wales TUC had been resolved so, too, had the debate over devolution. What is not in doubt is that Wales took a long step down the devolution road with the winning of the Wales TUC.

Welsh politics, more than most, are tidal. During the late 1960s the devolution tide was running strong in Wales with a series of Plaid Cymru-dominated by-elections — in Carmarthen, Caerphilly and the Rhondda — reflecting an almost tangibly changing mood. But after the 1970 general election the tide and the mood began to recede. So much so that devolutionists inside the Labour Party in Wales began to find it more difficult to hold their ground.

In 1973 the Kilbrandon Commission on the Constitution, set up by he Labout government in 1969 in the wake of nationalist by-election successes, reported in favour of elected Assemblies for Wales and Scotland. However, this did little immediately to revive the issue. This was only achieved after the February 1974 election when the small majority of the newly elected Labour government combined with the arrival of two nationalist MPs from Wales (for Meirionydd and Caernarfon) and seven from Scotland to place devolution once more at the forefront of the political agenda. But soon there was a backlash in Parliament. When the government began to frame its legislation it ran into stiff opposition from many of its own backbenchers, not least some from Wales. At this point, during 1975-6, it was the Wales TUC that proved influential in holding the line and ensuring that Welsh proposals were alongside those from Scotland when the full-scale Parliamentary debate on devolution opened. The Wales TUC provided a new dimension. For the first time in history Welsh aspirations were institutionalised on the broad base of the productive capacity of the people of Wales, giving a previously unknown durability to those aspirations.

The Wales TUC was born in conflict, between grassroots Welsh trade unionists and the establishment organisations of unionism in Wales, in particular the North and South Wales Regional Advisory Committees of the British TUC. When this establishment had been won, or by-passed, there was a fresh conflict between the new Welsh trade union establishment and the union establishment at the British level.

The idea of a Wales TUC was canvassed many times between 1945 and 1970. The main pressure came from the trades councils and their county federations. A significant step was made in 1960 when a South Wales Liaison Committee of trades councils was created. This proved a focal point for pressure for the Wales TUC. In 1966 the South Wales miners, in conference, unanimously approved proposals for a Wales TUC. At this stage, however, opposition came from north Wales. For example, Tom Jones, the Shotton-based leader of the Transport and General Workers' Union said:

> Our main objection is that it would impractical to organise as Wales is just not an economic unit. Trade unions and industries in North and South Wales are totally different and have completely different problems.[10]

Even so the debate had now reached a point sufficient to arouse strong opposition from the centre. In June 1968 George Woodcock, then General Secretary to the British TUC, was quoted as saying:

> A Welsh TUC would only arise if there was a Welsh government and a Welsh Confederation of Employers.[11]

A year later a highly significant organisational change was undertaken by the Transport and General Workers Union which replaced its separate North and South Wales structures with a single all-Wales organisation. The new structure gave the union a stronger base in Wales on which to rest a full-time secretariat. At the same time the change had an unintended, but wide-ranging impact. It removed at a stroke the foundation of the separate North and South Wales Regional Advisory Committees of the British TUC. Moreover, there was a growing appreciation of the development of Welsh politics amongst rank and file trade union membership. The late D. Ivor Davies, long-time Chairman of the Glamorgan Trades Council Federation, and later (in the mid-1970s) Chairman of the Wales TUC, recalled:

> It became clear that the leaders of the old Regional Advisory Committees were not really grappling with the problems of Wales. They wanted to concentrate on the problems of their own unions. But the establishment of the Secretary of State for Wales and the Welsh Office symbolised a developing awareness of nationhood amongst the people. In this situation the trade union movement was at a disadvantage.[12]

At the same time as the unification of the Transport and General Workers' Union organisation on an all-Wales basis its leadership passed to younger, more dynamic, and English hands. Doubtless they were less inhibited because of that. George Wright, the new general secretary and first secretary of the Wales TUC, had been brought up on disputes in the car industry in the Midlands. Through his initiative the Welsh Transport Union formed an axis with the Welsh Miners who had long supported a Wales TUC. Early in 1972 they jointly decided to establish a Wales TUC.

This was a unilateral decision made in the face of opposition from the London-based British TUC. During 1972 an organising committee was formed, embracing representatives from a dozen unions in Wales and the Trades Councils, a constitution was drawn up, and an inaugural conference organised at Llandrindod in February 1973. This conference, attended by 250 delegates from throughout Wales, was held in defiance of an instruction issued by leaders of the British TUC. They said that Welsh unionists should wait until the regional structure of the TUC in England and Wales could be considered as a whole. The North Wales Advisory Committee of the TUC supported the conference. But the South Wales Advisory Committee did not and many delegates attended in defiance of the rulings of their own union leadership. The draft constitution of the new Wales TUC was moved by the Transport Union's Welsh regional Secretary-designate, George Wright, who declared:

> I recognise, as an Englishman, that Wales is geographically separated. It has a separate culture, a separate people, and a separate language, and it has special problems. We intend to defend Wales against the economic and social neglect of the last fifty years.[13]

He was supported by Dai Francis, Welsh Secretary of the NUM who became the first Chairman of the Wales TUC and its most inspirational leader in the early years. Certainly, the creation of the Wales TUC had an immediate and powerful impact on the politics of devolution. At its second conference, in May 1973, it overwhelmingly passed a resolution calling for the establishment of a Welsh Assembly with legislative powers. This was a more radical position than the Labour party's policy which was for an Assembly with only executive powers. In terms of practical politics, over the next few years, the Wales TUC's position served to make Labour's proposals appear modest.

But quite apart from its specific support for a strong Welsh Assembly, the Wales TUC had a far deeper impact. It ensured that henceforward Welsh politics would also embrace the Welsh economy. As a result the devolution argument became more broadly based. The acceptance of the economic unity of Wales and the idea of a distinctive economy, with its own special needs and problems was a critical moment in the emergence of a separate Welsh politics in the mid twentieth century. It was also a prerequisite for the politics of devolution.

THE CAMPAIGN FOR AN ASSEMBLY

Intermittently since the 1950s, the devolution debate has been stimulated by a cross-party campaign outside the mainstream Labour movement. It was instructive that in the wake of the 1987 general election the Campaign for a Welsh Assembly — dormant since the 1979 referendum — was re-activated by Labour, Plaid Cymru and Liberal Democrat activists in the Cardiff Central constituency. This was significant for two reasons: first because the initiative came from southern, English-speaking Wales, albeit from within the nation's capital; but significant, too, because it came about as a result of a particular electoral outcome. In the general election the Conservative candidate in Cardiff Central, Ian Grist, retained his seat with a minority 37 per cent as a result of a close split of the vote between his two main rivals, Jon Owen Jones for Labour with 32 per cent, and Michael German for the Liberal Democrats, with 29 per cent. The lesson was taken that if the main opposition forces combined to at least some extent there would a greater chance of defeating a common enemy. In Cardiff Central a decision was made to combine around the issue of Welsh democracy.

Jon Owen Jones led a cross-party organising committee and over a year twenty campaign groups were established throughout Wales. In November 1988 a meeting to launch the Campaign was held in Merthyr Tydfil, not, for once, Llandrindod Wells. A Campaign Council was elected comprising 15 members of the Labour Party, six members of the Liberal Democrats, five members of Plaid Cymru, four members of the then still-existing Welsh Communist Party, one Wales Green Party member and four others with no party allegiance. Jon Owen Jones was elected chairman with two vice-chairmen, Geraint Howells, then Liberal Democrat MP for Ceredigion, and David Morris, MEP for South West Wales.

The manifesto of the new Campaign was, in effect, drawn up by the historian who prefers to be known as the people's remembrancer, Gwyn A Williams. In a typically emotional and rousing address at the Merthyr meeting he called for a 'Welsh Perestroika' (the time was pregnant with the momentous events unfolding in Eastern Europe). The essential, and most difficult requirement, he said, was unity across the parties around the democratic and elementary principle that the people of Wales should control their own affairs — 'We as a people have been around for two thousand years,' he said. 'Isn't it time we got the key to our own front door?' He warned, however that it would be no easy task, and went on to state the guiding principles:

> We do not have the independent history of the Scots; our history has been a history of internal division, internal fragmentation which has often left us helpless ... People say Wales is a nebulous concept. This is non-

> sense, it's no more nebulous than an idea of England. What is poisonous is the capitalist definition of Wales by regions defined according to capitalist convenience. That definition defines us out of existence. There is a higher law than the law of the market: it is the law of survival, of communal survival. We have a border in Wales. No-one proposes to make it a Berlin Wall but it exists. Everything west of that line in Wales, everyone west of that line who commits herself or himself to Wales is a member of the Welsh people. I don't care what language they speak. I don't care what colour their faces are, I don't care where they come from. If they live in Wales and commit themselves to Wales, they are Welsh people. And it is the elementary democratic right of that Welsh people to take possession of their own country, to elect in full democracy an assembly which will take over the Welsh state which already exists in embryo and will exercise as much self-government as is humanly possible within the new Europe in which we will take our place.[14]

The main impact of these early years of the re-established Campaign — it inherited a £100 bank balance from the Wales for the Assembly cross-party organisation formed to fight the 1979 referendum — was to be part of the pressure that revived the debate inside the Welsh Labour Party. During the early 1980s the issue had remained dormant. The party was still recovering from the damaging divisions that had occurred during the 1970s and did not want to re-open the debate. More to the point the leadership after 1983 fell into the hands of Neil Kinnock who had led the Labour Vote No Campaign in 1979.

In the wake of a third general election defeat in 1987 the question of the Welsh democratic deficit was cautiously pushed back on to the agenda of Welsh Labour conferences. Following year-long consultations by the Welsh executive a 'Welsh Regional Council' was suggested to take over the Welsh Office and the Quangos. By the time of the 1992 general election, Neil Kinnock notwithstanding, an elected Assembly was once more on offer.

During the election campaign the Campaign for a Welsh Assembly placed advertisements in the *Western Mail* and *Daily Post*, signed and paid for by a thousand supporters. Its main demand was for a constitutional conference to be called by the political parties and other representative organisations in the wake of the election to plan and timetable a Parliamentary Bill to create an Assembly. The initiative was rejected by the Welsh Labour Party executive, which said:

> Our victory in the election will represent a mandate from the Welsh people to implement our manifesto pledge (of a Welsh Assembly in the lifetime of a full Parliament). We do not accept the Campaign for a Welsh Assembly's apparent belief that a constitutional convention is a necessary prerequisite to legislation.[15]

Within weeks of the election defeat the Wales TUC, meeting in its conference at Tenby passed a resolution calling for a Welsh Constitutional Convention to be established along the lines of the cross-party Scottish Convention that had agreed proposals for a Scottish Parliament between 1989 and 1992. The Campaign for a Welsh Assembly responded by attempting to bring together representatives from key organisations such as the political parties, the churches, the local authority organisations, and the Wales TUC itself to draw up a framework document out of which a Convention might emerge. However, by August the Welsh Labour Executive had resolved to have nothing to do with outside organisations. Instead it established its own Constitutional Commission, chaired by the Rhondda constituency secretary Ken Hopkins.

THE CAMPAIGN FOR A PARLIAMENT

One response of the Campaign for a Welsh Assembly to this, by now traditional, rebuff from the Welsh Labour establishment was to re-focus its objectives by calling for a Parliament rather than an Assembly. At one level this was merely a matter of presentation rather than substance. From the time of its launch in 1988, the Campaign had specified in its constitution that its sole objective should be to achieve the widest possible agreement in favour of 'a legislative Assembly or Parliament with such powers as the people of Wales desire'.[16]

The key word in this formulation was *legislative*. However, the change of name, approved after a postal survey and overwhelming endorsement by the membership during 1993 — was of some symbolic importance. The intention was to signal a break with the devolution politics of the 1970s. While the 1978 Wales Act was regarded as a progressive measure, there was a strong feeling that it had been fundamentally flawed because it failed to provide a body with effective legislative and financial powers. This was the view of all leading figures in the Campaign from the start, including many in its leadership who were Labour Party members.

However, the change of name was undoubtedly controversial. Those who were against devolution, or only in favour of an Assembly with limited powers, now argued that the Campaign had moved in a natinalist direction. Others took a more robust view, arguing that if Labour's policy was to be credible it had to be intellectually coherent. The case for legislative powers was to give an Assembly or Parliament effective control over the Welsh Office's wide-ranging functions and budget. In effect, this argument was conceded by Labour's Policy Commission when it reported in May 1995 (see Chapter 1). In that case not to allow at least an element of financial autonomy was a recipe for instability. To separate tax spending from tax raising threatens real profligacy in public expenditure decisions, by separating power from responsibility.

Those arguing this inside the Welsh Labour Party were greatly strengthened by the Scottish Labour Party which for some years had been co-operating with the Liberal Democrats, the Green Party, the Scottish TUC, the churches, local authorities and other representatives from Scottish civil society inside the Scottish Convention. There agreement was being reached on legislative powers, fiscal competence, and proportional representation for a Scottish Parliament.[17]

As a result many Labour supporters were among the 250 people who attended the Constitutional Conference organised by the Parliament for Wales Campaign at Llandrindod in March 1994. Those who attended also included representatives from many local authorities, trade unions, churches and many other organisations. A *Democracy Declaration* was approved (see Appendix, p.187) which was later submitted as a petition to the European Parliament by the Campaign's Vice-Chair, David Morris MEP.

The conference registered a landmark in Welsh politics. A strong intellectual case for legislative and financial powers for a Parliament was made, as well as internal democracy in its elections and procedures.[18] The arguments for proportional representation and the need to provide equality for women were especially salient and established important markers that were, in short order, taken up by supporters within the Welsh Labour Party.

SUSTAINABLE DEVELOPMENT

The most remarkable result of the 1992 general election in Wales took place in Ceredigion and Pembroke North. In a local alliance with the Green Party, Plaid Cymru came from fourth position in 1987 — behind Labour, Conservatives and the Liberal Democrats — to win the seat. There was a 13 per cent electoral swing in the vote from the Liberal Democrats to Plaid Cymru.

The fusion between Plaid Cymru and the Green Party in Ceredigion and Pembroke North was undoubtedly part of the explanation for this dramatic electoral shift. Personalities, of course, played their part. However, the new MP Cynog Dafis was swift to acknowledge that the collaboration between the two parties had provided an essential dynamic. As he said, it 'did far more than merely combining the existing, or even potential support of the two parties separately'.[19]

The collaboration between the two parties was highly controversial amongst the Greens, especially outside the constituency. Subsequently there was much internal argument and a lot of pressure until, in 1995, formal links between the two parties in the constituency were broken. Nonetheless, in the intervening years an important democratic movement in Welsh politics was initiated, forging a creative alliance between democracy and the environment that promises to have a long-lasting impact. It was given expression in a joint Manifesto, issued six months after the election by Plaid Cymru and the Ceredigion and Pembroke North Green Party. Their alliance, they said, was based on three principles:

> First we need to find ways to live in harmony with our natural environment. Secondly that we take back control of our lives through achieving genuine local democracy and the establishment of a Parliament for

> Wales. and through the development of a more self-reliant economy. Thirdly we want a social order whose priority is a decent quality of life for all our people in the context of our global responsibilities. This includes the celebration of diversity, of place, culture, language and lifestyle ...
>
> At the heart of our problem is a runaway super-industrialism of huge and complex organisations, whether public or private. There is a growing loss of a human scale of things and the sense of personal responsibility that goes with it. Increasingly, one place feels much like any other as the diversity of human environments, lifestyles, culture and language, all diminish. How much are we willing to lose forever in exchange for a never-ending consumerism? An increasing number of people are making this three-cornered connection: between the need, first, for a Green economy; second, taking back control of our future both in Wales and our communities; and, third, that here is the only effective way left to resist a deep-rooted Thatcherism which is particularly alien to Wales and has proved hugely destructive, as the number of unemployed and desperate soars.[20]

Given its west Wales origins this document, *Towards a Green Welsh Future*, naturally places a good deal of emphasis on the needs of a rural communities. It has sections dealing with farming — and especially the predicament of the small family farm — and the problems of small businesses in a rural setting. Ever present, however is a wider Welsh, European and global context. The European dimension is seen as especially relevant:

> We see the future of Wales as not merely another nation-state, but as fighting for, and part of, a Europe of the Regions, as the only alternative to a Europe of the transnationals and the bureaucrats. The European Community should only exercise the (relatively few) powers that really have to be exercised at an all-Europe level. And those powers must be exercised by a fully democratic Parliament, which includes a Second House directly representing regions and small nations like Wales. For us, Europe means power passing to Cardiff and directly to Welsh communities as well as to Strasbourg.
>
> Wales is in fact a very diverse country; on many different issues people in Gwent would be inclined to see things differently from Gwynedd. Provided certain

> overall citizen rights are safeguarded each community should be enabled to live in its own way within a Welsh Confederation, much as the Swiss do in their cantons. At a local level people must be empowered to take maximum practical responsibility for their community well-being. In particular we favour a strong dose of direct democracy (councillor recall, local referenda and the like), combined with proportional representation for all elected bodies.[21]

These ideas, blending the radical impulses of two parties and two different traditions, proved a powerful mobilising force. Elsewhere in Wales in the 1992 general election there was a political stand-off. By and large the people of Wales voted *against* the Tories rather than *for* any movement for change. In Ceredigion and Pembroke North, however, things were different.

CThe constituency is, of course, highly individual, a region within Wales in its own right. With around 60 per cent of its population Welsh-speaking it is an integral part of the Welsh heartland — Y Fro Gymraeg — that Plaid Cymru has made its own since the 1960s. The bedrock of Plaid Cymru's support is the constituency's hill farmers who further north, in Gwynedd, have also been a foundation of the party's strength since the 1960s. In Ceredigion they continued through the 1980s to vote Liberal Democrat, mainly out of sentiment and in support of one of their number, the former MP (now Lord) Geraint Howells. In truth, however, they were always as much nationalist in outlook as Liberal and Geraint Howells reflected that in the unwavering support he gave to the Welsh language and a Parliament for Wales.

His stance held the line until the 1990s, by which time the farmers were in crisis. Over ten years their average annual income had more than halved, from a little over £22,000 to just £10,000. At the same time the number of farms for rent dropped steeply and the price of land doubled.[22] They were angry, especially with the Tories with whom some of them had supported in the early 1980s, and were looking for more aggressive leadership. This was provided by Plaid Cymru's Cynog Dafis who, even by the standards of Welsh politics is an unusual figure, ideally formed to create an alliance with the Green Party. A schoolteacher in the constituency, Dafis cut his political teeth on the direct action campaigns of Cymdeithas yr Iaith Gymraeg in the

1960s and 1970s. He was the author of its 1972 Manifesto, a landmark document that made an important distinction between violence to property and violence to the person.[23] Cymdeithas yr Iaith's success, especially in the campaign for S4C, owed a great deal to that sensitivity.

By the 1980s in Ceredigion and Pembroke North it was sorely needed. Here was the flash point for one of the most potentially dangerous issues in Welsh politics, the in-migration of hundreds (approaching thousands) of young English people, out-bidding the indigenous Welsh in the property market, and changing the linguistic balance of many primary schools virtually overnight. Many of these people were moving into Wales in search of a more ecological way of life and were natural Green Party standard-bearers. They tended to be viewed with suspicion by the established population. In turn the incomers often found the indigenous Welsh not only linguistically unintelligible but a reservoir of a nationalism that some equated all too readily with racism.

That the political representatives of these two groups were brought together in harmonious co-operation over the two years preceding the 1992 general election was a triumph of hope over experience. As Cynog Dafis put it

> What we consciously decided to do was to set up an alliance between Welsh radical nationalists and English immigrants, and that is what we achieved — as a challenge to the old, establishment, inert, inward-looking, negative politics of the Cardiganshire Liberals that in a way is equivalent to the Labourism of the Valleys. It was an astonishing psychological phenomenon and a complete mystery to the Labour Party. After all, in their outlook Welsh nationalists are supposed to hate the English.[24]

A more lasting legacy of this episode was the injection of a sophisticated environmental agenda into Welsh economic policy-making, as an essential building block for Welsh democracy. The idea of 'sustainable development' — economic development which is not at the expense of future generations — took hold. At Westminster Cynog Dafis recruited a Green Party researcher, Victor Anderson, and together they set about producing a *Sustainable Development Strategy for Wales*, published in 1995-6.[25]

In line with the thinking behind the 1992 United Nations Earth Summit at Rio de Janeiro, this document represented the beginning of a movement towards integrating the needs of the Welsh economy with those of the environment, a project that will be an on-going preoccupation for the Welsh democracy movement.

THE CHANGING FACE OF WALES

Since an Assembly or Parliament for Wales was last on the agenda, in the 1970s, the Welsh economy, culture and political landscape have all altered significantly and in a very short space of time. A new generation is coming of age in a Wales that is changing under their feet. The backbone of the economy, for instance, is still heavy industry, but one that instead of being in decline is now at the forefront of European technology. In 1994 Wales produced more steel than ever before in its history but with many fewer workers. In 1970 some 55,000 workers in the industry produced 4 million tons of steel. In 1994 just 15,000 workers produced more than 5 million tons.

This fundamental change, together with the virtual disappearance of coal mining, has provided the backcloth for a renaissance in the manufacturing and service industries, stimulated to a great extent by inward investment, as described in Chapter 6. There has undoubtedly been an accompanying large-scale dislocation in terms of job losses and redundancy for many, especially older men, while many women have entered full and part-time paid work. Overall, however, the changes have had a positive, modernising and transforming impact.

A consensus of forecasters see Wales as growing significantly faster than the UK average in the second half of the 1990s, led by a strong manufacturing performance. Gross domestic product (GDP) in Wales is expected to grow by an average of 3.6% a year to the end of the decade, compared with a UK average of 3%. Gradually, Wales is catching up with the more prosperous English Regions, in particular the South East, East Anglia and the South West. Planners at the Welsh Development Agency have identified seven main reasons:

* *Export orientation of manufacturing industry*: which lessens the dependence of Wales on the UK economy

and its fluctuations, with Wales increasingly dependent on markets in mainland Europe (and beyond).

* *Diversification*: Wales is substantially less dependent on the traditional heavy industries, which were in turn so dependent on the stage of the economic cycle. Whilst steel remains important to Wales, its increasing export ratio make it (and hence Wales) less reliant on volatile UK consumer spending.

* *Manufacturing performance*: productivity growth in Wales has been spectacular, pushing unit labour costs to amongst Britain's (and Europe's) lowest, giving Wales a vital competitive edge.

* *Feminisation*: by the end of 1995 women were more than half of all employees in Wales; increases in female participation have substantially increased Wales' productive capacity.

* *Inward investment*: Wales continues to attract a relatively high share of new foreign investment, both a cause and effect of increasing Welsh manufacturing performance.

* *Coal*: the virtual demise of the coal industry in Wales has released one constraint on Welsh economic growth; in the past this has tended to be offset by the decline of the coal industry.

* *Steel*: the market for strip steel products (produced in Wales) is very buoyant, with output growth fed by continued productivity improvement and price rises which have restored profitability in steel production.[26]

This analysis holds out the prospects for a buoyant Welsh economy in the coming decade, in contrast to the difficult economic period of the 1970s when the last devolutionary effort was mounted. All experience shows that people are much readier to contemplate political change in times of relative affluence, when there is greater security, than in times of relative hardship. It is no coincidence that the last major advance in Welsh institution-building, the creation of the Welsh Office, was during the 1960s , a time of comparative prosperity and also cultural and political change. The later 1990s promise to bring together a similar combination of circumstances.

Just as in the 1960s, the change will take place against a background experience of Wales being run for an extended period by a minority political party, the Conservatives. By itself this has had a radicalising impact, especially on the Welsh Labour Party. In the 1990s the position is starker than in the 1960s. In the 1994 European elections, for instance, the Conservatives slipped into fourth place, behind the Liberal Democrats and Plaid Cymru as well as Labour, with just 14.6 per cent of the poll.

In the 1960s, when Labour came to power the Welsh Office did not exist and the administration of Wales by a minority political force was not so transparent. When the devolution debate last reached the salience it has today, in the 1970s, the Welsh Office did exist, and so did many Quangos. But in those days this governing apparatus was run by the Labour Party. At the time of the 1979 referendum the attitude of many Labour councillors, Labour placemen and placewomen on the Quangos, and many Labour MPs and constituency activists was quite simply: 'We're already running the show, why change?' Now, however, this outlook has been undermined by four lost general elections and nearly two decades of Conservative rule.

The point leads to a second seismic shift in the Welsh political landscape in the 1990s, discussed in Chapter 3. This is the reorganisation of local government with the twenty-two new unitary authorities that replace the eight counties and thirty-seven districts in April 1996. As argued, this change amounts to a formidable attack on local democracy and local power. The present eight counties have a fair chance of operating as strategic authorities in the areas of their main responsibility — education, social services, planning and highways. Twenty-two authorities will be ill-equipped to do the same. They will be forced into complex arrangements by creating joint boards and lead authorities in many areas of administration. We will see a new two-tier structure emerge, only one of which will be directly elected, with the other indirectly elected.

There is a paradox in all of this, however, since the reorganisation is highly beneficial for the devolution movement. All Opposition parties are agreed that a single tier of around twenty-five authorities would work best below an all-Wales Assembly or Parliament. So the present reorganisation, in that sense, is paving the way. In that case, it might be asked, why did the Tories do it? They could perhaps have held the line with a single tier of eight authorities, based on the existing county councils. This was the course of action advocated by the Wales CBI.

Instead, the Conservatives are helping put in place the building blocks of a devolved Wales. Why they are allowing this contradiction to happen is one of the more intriguing questions of contemporary Welsh politics.

A third shift in the Welsh landscape in the 1990s is, of course, the European Union. This new horizon was barely visible in the 1950s, and its outlines were only beginning to emerge in the 1970s. In the 1990s, however, it is coming more and more to dominate the scene as discussed in the previous two chapters. Quite simply it has transformed the terms of the argument. Whereas in the 1970s it was possible for the opponents of devolution to argue with some credibility about the dangers of separatism and slippery slopes towards it, the evolving European framework has fatally undermined the attack. Even such Right-wing thinkers as Ferdinand Mount — a disciple of the greatest English Conservative of recent times, Michael Oakeshott — now urges support for Welsh and Scottish Assemblies, arguing that :'the encircling European girdle makes the UK *safe* for devolution' [his italics].[27]

Writing in 1949 of the devolution movements over the previous three-quarters of a century, Sir John Rees, who had been Principal of University College, Cardiff for twenty years, remarked that it was:

> ... interesting to notice that each successive movement for a fuller recognition of the needs of Wales has achieved some result, though it has been by no means commensurate with the effort, or indeed directly related to the demand.[28]

Thus the Cymru Fydd movement of the 1880s and 1890s had not achieved Home Rule, but what did come out of the period was the 1889 Welsh Intermediate Education Act, the establishment of the University Colleges of Wales, the National Library and National Museum, and later the Welsh Board of Education (1907) and Health (1909), and the Disestablishment of the Church in Wales (1920). As we have seen, the Parliament for Wales Campaign of the 1950s provided part of the background for the creation of the Welsh Office and Secretary of State in 1964. Pressure for an elected Assembly in the 1960s resulted in a greater elaboration of the Welsh administrative machine, in particular the creation of the Welsh Development Agency in 1975.

Can we expect another, unexpected consequence to result from the campaign in the 1990s, perhaps some kind of advance but once again falling short of the main aspiration? One answer is to say that it is difficult to imagine what kind of advance, short of a democratic one, would now be possible. What is certainly the case is that as we have moved through the second half of the twentieth century the political landscape has shifted in favour of the pro-devolutionists.

CONTRADICTING A CULTURE OF DEFEAT

Yet any contemplation of a democratic advance for Wales in the 1990s cannot ignore the reality of what happened in 1979. In a typically cryptic remark, Saunders Lewis wrote shortly before the vote ,'We are asked to tell the Government on St David's Day whether we want a Welsh Assembly or not. The implied question is: 'Are you a nation or not?'[29] Writing some years afterwards I reflected that it was possible to explain the result in terms of the unpopularity of the Government of the day, or as a rejection of what was seen as another layer of expensive bureaucracy, rather than a denial by the people of Wales of their nationhood. Even so, I continued:

> ... history shows that the Welsh do seem to recoil instinctively whenever there is an opportunity to assert their national identity. It is as though Wales has lived too long in the shadow of a powerful English presence to risk brash adventure: much better to make progress quietly, by stealth.[30]

This is just another way of saying that for long generations the Welsh have lived in a culture of defeat, sometimes of resistance, but rarely of victory. Unlike the Scots, we have no memories of successful wars of independence and the experience of institution-building that ensued. Instead, we have memories of the death of Llywelyn ap Gruffudd on 11 December 1282 and the collapse of the embryonic Welsh state which he created. The record of his death in the chronicle *The Kings of the Saxons* concludes 'And then all Wales was cast to the ground'. In the greatest elegy lamenting Llywelyn's death Gruffudd ab yr Ynad

Coch, one of the Poets of the Princes, sees in the event signs of the end of the world.[31] Where politics is concerned that essential pessimism has remained with us ever since.

Raymond Williams often drew attention to this underlying reality of the Welsh condition. What are generally seen as distinctive Welsh institutions and impulses, such as Methodism or trade unionism, have more often than not been imported from England. Sometimes they have been translated into the Welsh situation with a passion and intensity that can be seen as distinctively Welsh. But, as Williams says,

> ... unless we relate it, at every point, to the long experience of defeat and subordination, we project a quite false essential autonomy.[32]

At the same time experience of defeat can be far from negative. Arguably people learn more from their defeats than their victories. It is arguable, too, that many Welsh characteristics we celebrate — warmth and intimacy, concern for the underdog, egalitarian values and the socialism arising out of Methodism — have come about not just as a result of the relatively small scale of our society, but also from a sense of solidarity in the common experience of defeat.

There have been two main responses. One has been resistance. The mythology around Owain Glyndwr exercises its power just because his campaign was essentially one of resistance. And it is noteworthy that another essential part of this particular myth is that Owain was never decisively defeated. He simply disappeared ... into legend. In modern times resistance has ranged from the Merthyr Rising and the Rebecca riots to the more recent militant trade union struggles, especially involving the miners in 1926 and then, again, in 1984-5. Invariably this real resistance — real in terms of really felt memory — has ended in defeat, but defeat qualified by dignity amidst despair, and celebrated because of that.

The second response has been to become involved, to an extent out of all proportion to our size and population, in radical English or British movements, specifically Liberalism followed by Labourism. In each case the original impulse was one of local militancy — the land question in nineteenth century Wales, the syndicalist class struggles of early twentieth century Wales —

but always followed by incorporation and containment, and the politics of demobilisation discussed in the opening Chapter. This experience has often been accompanied by a rejection of the Welsh dimension as backward-looking and parochial in which, as Williams has it,

> ... the confident imperatives of incorporation — a transforming Liberalism, a redeeming and transforming Labourism — are repeated long after they have practically failed, both at the centre and in Wales itself. ... [The rejections] have typically included, also, a particular spitefulness against all or any countervailing Welsh specificities; a distinguishing Welsh form of anti-Welshness, finding only partial and insufficient excuse in the excesses of romantic nationalism. It is within these negative forms of the central complexities that much of the surface politics of contemporary Wales is still conducted, and the negative effects have to be reckoned as still predominant (as the referendum on devolution so damagingly showed).[33]

These psychological complexes of the Welsh are well understood by the historian Kenneth O. Morgan. So much so that when he was completing his history of Twentieth Century Wales, within months of the 1979 referendum, he still felt able to give it the title *Rebirth of a Nation.* In the final pages he refers to the American historian, C. Vann Woodward, who wrote that during the twentieth century the southern States have been more in tune with the national experience of America than those of the North:

> The South had known the bitterness of military defeat in the Civil War, and of psychological disillusion in the Reconstruction that followed it, and the need to cling, almost in despair, to old values and to rebuild a shattered society. To the United States generally — in the aftermath of the slump and mass unemployment after 1929, the pressures of the Cold War in the forties, and the internal crises of conscience such as racial disturbances and the war in Vietnam in the sixties — the perspective and experiences of the South were especially valuable.[33]

Kenneth O Morgan goes on to quote C. Vann Woodward again in that 'history was something that had happened' to the South in a painful way. History has often been painful for Wales. In the later twentieth century, however, history has likewise also 'happened' to the English, especially in terms of identity problems. As imperial Britain declined the Welsh could take some comfort in that their social culture was still flourishing as a living and distinctive part of the European world.

In the 1990s the American Welsh poet Jon Dressel was much influenced by this reference in *Rebirth of a Nation* to the parallels between the historic and cultural experience of defeat suffered by Wales and the American South. It prompted him to write a thirty-three part dramatic narrative *The Road to Shiloh*.[35] In an exposition of how he approached this task Dressel refers to his experience of Wales and especially the 1979 referendum:

> I began to ask myself something like this: just what was the relationship between my experience of Wales and my sense of American identity, and how had Wales made me a different kind of American than I had been before? The answer that finally came back was that the only sense of national identity that is worth a plugged nickel is one which can face, and transcend, the experience of defeat.[36]

In Wales we have been facing and transcending defeat for generations. The fact that a Parliament for Wales is now once more on the agenda, less than two decades after 1979, is another testimony to that. More and more people in Wales are coming to see its urgent need. As I write, in the summer of 1995, some, perhaps unlikely, allies are swelling our ranks. A Wales CBI survey among business leaders in Wales shows support for devolution to be at an all-time high.[37] The Archbishop of Wales, the Most Reverend Alwyn Rice Jones, in a speech at the National Eisteddfod, says:

> I believe the time has come for the Government to acknowledge there is now a general consensus for a measure of independence and experience of self-government.[38]

There is evidence within the Welsh Labour Party that the politics of demobilisation that held it in thrall for more than a decade after 1979 are beginning to unravel. The new campaign, Welsh Labour Action is calling for legislative powers, financial autonomy, equal representation for men and women, and a fair voting system for an Assembly. As it says:

> Labour are already promising all this to the people of Scotland and not to the people of Wales. Do the people of Wales deserve second best?[39]

So there is hope for the future. And that hope represents a prospect for resolving many of the contradictions of Welsh politics. At last we have a chance of turning a culture of defeat into one of self-reliance and optimism. At last we have the opportunity of transforming a society of British subjects into a nation of Welsh European citizens.

NOTES

1. Quoted in Robert Griffiths, *S.O. Davies - A Socialist Faith* (Llandysul: Gomer, 1983), pp.170-1.
2. *Ibid.*
3. *Ibid.*
4. James Griffiths, *Pages from Memory* (London: Dent, 1969), p.162.
5. See Robert Griffiths, 'The Other Aneurin Bevan', *Planet* No. 41, January 1978.
6. See Gwyn Jenkins, 'Keeping up with the Macs - The Devolution Debate of 1957-59', in *Planet* No 82, August 1990, for a full account of this episode. What follows is based on Gwyn Jenkins' research on the papers of J. Idwal Jones MP at the Clwyd Record Office, Ruthun.
7. Huw T. Edwards, *Hewn From The Rock* (Cardiff: Western Mail & TWW Ltd., 1967), p.160.
8. Richard Crossman, *Diaries of a Cabinet Minister*, Vol. 1, Minister of Housing 1964-66 (London: Cape, 1975), p.117.
9. James Griffiths, 'Welsh Politics in My Lifetime' (1973) in *James Griffiths and His Times* (Labour Party Wales, 1 Cathedral Road, Cardiff, 1975), p.47. See also the *Western Mail*, 8 May 1976: 'The Resignation that saved the Welsh Office'.
10. *Western Mail*, 6 December 1966.
11. *Western Mail*, 4 June 1968.
12. Interview with the author, October 1976.
13. Quoted in the *Morning Star*, 12 February 1973.
14. The full text is carried in a pamphlet published by the Campaign, *Agreeing an Assembly for the 1990s*, August 1989. This also contains a critique of the Welsh Labour Party's Assembly proposals of that year.
15. *Western Mail*, 2 April 1992. This edition of the paper also carried the Campaign's two-page advertisement, under the heading 'Let's Make It Happen'.
16. See the Campaign's evidence to the Welsh Labour Party's Constitutional Commission, *Empowering the People*, October 1994, avail-

able from the Parliament for Wales Campaign, 11 Gordon Road, Cardiff.
17. See the final report from the Scottish Convention, October 1995, available from Roseberry Hpouse, 9 Haymarket Terrace, Edinburgh, EH12 5XZ.
18. See John Osmond (ed.) *A Parliament for Wales* (Llandysul: Gomer, 1994).
19. Cynog Dafis MP in *Towards a Green Welsh Future* (Plaid Cymru and Green Party Ceredigion and Pembroke North, December 1992), p.1.
20. *Ibid.* p.2.
21. *Ibid.* p.3 .
22. See John Osmond, 'Looking After Our Land - Farming and a Welsh Parliament' in John Osmond (ed.) *A Parliament for Wales* (Llandysul: Gomer, 1994).
23. Cynog Dafis *Maniffesto Cymdeithas yr Iaith Gymraeg* 1972, translated by Harri Webb as 'Cymdeithas yr Iaith — the Manifesto' in *Planet* No 26/27, Winter 1974-5.
24. Interview with the author, October 1992.
25. *Sustainable Development Strategy for Wales*, published by Plaid Cymru as a draft consultation document, July 1995.
26. Welsh Development Agency, *Interim Report of the Regional Technology Plan for Wales*, June 1995.
27. Ferdinand Mount, *The British Constitution Now* (London: Heinemann, 1992), pp.197-205.
28. J.F. Rees, *The Problem of Wales, in Nineteenth Century and After*, 1949, reprinted as the title essay in his volume of essays *The Problem of Wales* (Cardiff: University of Wales Press, 1963). As a new footnote to the essay, in 1963, he adds, 'It has been suggested that a plebiscite might be organised to ascertain what the people of Wales want. That assumes that they know what they want. It might prove a serious fiasco.'
29. Saunders Lewis, letter to the *Western Mail*, 26 February 1979.
30. John Osmond, 'The Dynamic of Institutions' in *The National Question Again* (Llandysul: Gomer, 1985), p. 254.
31. See Gwyn Thomas's foreword to a 700th anniversary publication of Gruffudd ab yr Ynad Coch's elegy by Gwasg Grygynog in 1982 (a limited edition in which the English translation is by Joseph P. Clancy). The translated lines begin

> Heart cold in the breast with dread,
> Grief-stricken for a king ...
> .... See you not that the world is ending/
> Ah, God, that the sea would cover the land!

Writing of Llywellyn the journalist Mario Basini reflected that '... small nations striving to make their way in a hostile world need their heroic failures ... after 700 years the memory of the last native Prince of Wales remains as fresh as a newly opened wound for many of his modern fellow countrymen.' (*Western Mail*, 14 August 1995).
32. Raymond Williams, 'Wales and England' in John Osmond (ed.) *The National Question Again* (Llandysul: Gomer, 1985), p.24.

33. *Ibid.*, p.28.
34. Kenneth O Morgan, *Rebirth of a Nation: Wales 1880-1980* (Oxford: Oxford University Press, 1981), p.420.
35. Jon Dressel, *The Road to Shiloh* (Llandysul: Gomer, 1994). Shiloh was the scene of a great American Civil War battle fought in southern Tennessee in 1862 .
36. Jon Dressel, 'Living with Defeat - The Road to Shiloh', *New Welsh Review* No 23, winter 93-4, p.22.
37. 'Business support for Assembly rises', *Western Mail*, 25 July 1995. A poll carried out by the Wales Chamber of Commerce and Industry and reported in the August 1995 issue of its magazine *Business in Wales* , found 79 per cent responding positively to the question 'Will a Welsh Assembly be beneficial to business?'
38. 'Archbishop in Plea for Home Rule', *Western Mail*, 9 August 1995.
39. Welsh Labour Action, *Campaign for a Real Assembly*, leaflet issued at the 1995 Colwyn Bay National Eisteddfod.

Appendix

DEMOCRACY DECLARATION

AGREED BY THE LLANDRINDOD WELLS DEMOCRACY CONFERENCE, March 1994, BY THE ANNUAL GENERAL MEETING OF THE PARLIAMENT FOR WALES CAMPAIGN, LLANBADARN FAWR, June 1994, AND PRESENTED AS A PETITION TO THE EUROPEAN PARLIAMENT, October 1994

1) A Welsh Parliament will ensure that policies favoured by a majority of the people of Wales are followed. It will build a better future for our people by placing emphasis on economic regeneration and the provision of work. It will give us the freedom and responsibility to renew our culture and express our unity, national identity, and cultural diversity.

2) A Welsh Parliament will ensure, from the start, that there is a gender balance in its elected representatives, and will ensure that its procedures will enable women, men and minority groups to participate to the fullest extent.

3) The Parliament will be directly elected by a system of proportional representation.

4) The written and verbal proceedings of the Parliament will be conducted through the two main languages of Wales, Welsh and English.

5) The Parliament will take over all the powers and functions currently exercised by the Welsh Office and its Quangos (appointed bodies) and bring them under democratic control.

6) The Parliament will be able to make laws and determine taxes.

7) Amongst its responsibilities the Parliament will directly control job creation and the Welsh economy, the health service, housing, education, the environment, roads and transport, agriculture, the arts and culture, and local government. As things

are decisions on all these are made by the Welsh Office and the people the Secretary of State for Wales appoints to run the Quangos — the 80 unelected bodies like the Welsh Development Agency, Health Authorities, Education Funding Councils, Countryside Council, and Housing for Wales. This is a bureaucratic, undemocratic tier of Welsh government.

8) The Parliament will ensure that local authorities, and especially the Community Councils which are closest to the people, are strengthened. The powers and duties of each level of government will derive from the people and will be defined by the Welsh Parliament. These powers and duties will be in conformity with the general principle of subsidiarity.

9) Public and civil servants working for all tiers of government in Wales will belong to an integrated Welsh Public Service responsible to the Welsh Parliament.

10) The larger continental members of the European Union— including Germany, France, Spain, Italy and Belgium — all have elected Regional Governments. Their average size and population is 8,000 square miles and 3 million, very similar to the size and population of Wales. A Parliament will enable us to participate fully with the rest of the European Union and be properly represented on the Committee of the Regions set up by the Maastricht Treaty.

INDEX